MW00682289

*The Parables:*

# The Forgotten Message

## Hendrik van Tuyll

Middle Street Communications, Inc.

*The Parables:*
# The Forgotten Message

Copyright © 1993 by Hendrik van Tuyll

Printed in the United States of America

All rights reserved. No part of this book may be reproduced or transmitted in any form or by any means, electronic or mechanical, including photocopying and recording, or by any information storage or retreival system, except by written permission of the publisher.

Library of Congress Catalog Card Number: 92-61644
ISBN 0-9634068-4-1

 Middle Street Communications, Inc.
P. O. Box 223
Pelham, AL 35124-0223

Material from *Gistern, Vandaag en Morgen* by W. H. van de Pol (1979) used with permission of the publisher, Gooi en Sticht, Hilversum, Nederland.

**Publisher's Cataloging-in-Publication Data**

van Tuyll, Hendrik
      The Parables: The Forgotten Message

      Includes index.
      1. Jesus Christ—Parables.
2. Parables—History and Criticism. 3. Bible. N.T. Gospels—
Criticism interpretation, etc. 4. Bible—Theology
5. Philosophy and Religion.
I. Title
BT375.2V36    1993    226'.806    92-61644
ISBN 0-9634068-4-1    $9.95    Softcover

*The Parables:*
# The Forgotten Message

# CONTENTS

# I.

According to Matthew and Mark, Jesus spoke to the multitude in Parables only:

> All these things spake Jesus unto the multitude in parables; and without a parable spake he not unto them. (Matt. 13:34)

> But without a parable spake he not unto them... (Mark 4:34)

Yet throughout the history of Christianity very little attention has been paid to the Parables. The Parables have not had any influence on the formation of Christian doctrine. What is essential in Christian doctrine cannot be found in the Parables. What the Parables teach as being of the utmost importance, Christian doctrine does not mention.

Which picture, which understanding of the teachings of Jesus, will we get when we begin to realize what it means that Jesus spoke to the multitude in Parables only?

The gospels of Matthew, Mark, Luke and John unanimously agree that teaching was the most important part of the task of Jesus when He appeared before the multitude. In His Parables, however, Jesus never spoke about what, for the last 1,800 years, has been considered essential to the Christian faith. Nor did Jesus mention what were considered the essentials of the Jewish faith. These facts have been overlooked by the many different Christian churches.

On the discussion between the Church of Rome and the Churches of the Reformation, for example, the Parables have had no impact at all. What captivated the minds of Church thinkers at that time were the problems of how to interpret the sacraments, how to formulate the right faith, and what to do with those who would disagree. To this day the Christian faith has little in common with the content of the Parables. The Parables have become the stepchildren of Christianity. This perhaps made it possible for Christianity to become a conventional religion—and that forms a formidable obstacle for coming closer to the Parables.

We will see in this book, however, that the situation is even more complex. Explicitly Jesus has said that He spoke to the multitude in Parables in order *not* to be understood.

> Therefore I speak to them in parables: because they seeing see not; and hearing they hear not, neither do they understand. (Matt. 13:13)

> And he said unto them, Unto you is given to know the mystery of the kingdom of God: but unto them that are without, all these things are done in parables:
> That seeing they may see, and not perceive; and hearing they may hear, and not understand...
> (Mark 4:11-12)

> And he said, Unto you it is given to know the mysteries of the kingdom of God: but to others in parables; that seeing they might not see, and hearing they might not understand.  (Luke 8:10)

Confronting the Parables will make us realize that our own convictions, our truths, our outlook on life—which are just as conventional as those of the Jewish society of some 2,000 years ago—cannot be traced back to the Parables.

Through His teachings—for instance: judge not (Matt. 7:1)—and through His attitude towards men, Jesus made it clear that the attitude of man towards his fellow men has to be of a different, new, and higher order than that of the conventional morality of that time. Never has Jesus urged His disciples to condemn those who act wrongly. Has Jesus not asked His followers to forgive seventy times seven, even when evil had been committed against oneself (Matt. 18:22)?

It cannot be maintained that this teaching has been assimilated into our everyday morality, just as it was not assimilated into decisions of the Church to persecute those whose convictions differed from a majority of believers. With a profound seriousness, Christianity has endeavored to impose its beliefs on the multitude.[1]

---

[1]Always this approach has been in marked contrast with that of Jesus. Compare that conventional attitude with Anatole France's description of the character Jérôme Coignard: "He had arrived at the point where he believed that citizens only condemn such a large number of their peers to infamy in order to enjoy by contrast the pleasure of being held in esteem. It was this view which made him prefer bad company to the good at the example of Him who lived among the publicans and the prostitutes. There he kept the purity of heart, the gift of sympathy and the treasures of charity." (*Les Opinions de M. Jérôme Coignard*, Oeuvres Complètes de Anatole France, Paris, Calmann - Levy Editeurs, 1926, Tome VIII, p. 319) (translated by author). Both in doctrine and in lifestyle, Christian churches traditionally prefer to ignore this aspect of the Gospel.

Hand in hand with that attitude of judging and condemning goes the constant endeavor to quote words of Jesus only within a common framework of understanding. Sayings of Jesus which do not fit into the conventional framework of believing and understanding are ignored. Christianity has not focused its attention, for instance, on Matthew 5:48, "Be ye therefore perfect, even as your Father which is in heaven is perfect."

Christianity could only become the kind of conventional, organized religion it is now by failing to realize that the teachings of Jesus were not given to be selected by man and then put in the framework of Christian doctrine. But that has been done, and we may well wonder why. As the Nobel prize-winning author Anatole France once pointed out, without the instructions and doctrines of Christianity, the words of Jesus when quoted in the middle ages and later still seemed to be new and dangerous.

Because we have been conditioned to regard the Parables as impractical, they are never invoked for the solution to our manifold and vast problems. The simple idea to use the Parables to find these solutions would immediately be rejected. So little is the impact of the Parables, even their form has not been followed in the composing of sermons—although Jesus spoke to the multitude in Parables only. One can only conclude that the Parables are left aside just where they should have the greatest impact.

This situation is not new; this is not something of our own time only. The procedure of neglecting the Parables can already be found as early as the Epistles. If we had only the Epistles, what would we know about Jesus' teachings in

Parables? Nothing. We see the same extraordinary phenomenon of selective elimination in the Gospels. Although according to the Gospels the teachings of Jesus were of the greatest importance, few Parables have been inserted in the text of the Gospels—few compared to the very many Jesus must have pronounced. We might possibly suppose that the number of Parables was severely restricted by the authors of the Gospels to leave room for other information. But when we examine the Gospels we see that the Parables do not have the important part we might expect. We are then forced to take another step backwards and ask what was the attitude of the Apostles towards the Parables?

In Acts 15 we see that the Apostle Paul had a difference of understanding with the Apostles regarding the extent the Jewish laws had to be fulfilled by the converted Gentiles. Apparently Paul's attention was not drawn by the Apostles towards the Parables and, specifically, towards the fact that the Parables do not mention anything at all of Jewish laws or of a necessity of having to obey them. It seems a strange omission, given the circumstances, that the Apostles did not mention the Parables, the teachings of Jesus for the multitude.

The whole controversy between the Apostles and Paul seems to indicate that in their memories of Jesus the Parables had already receded into oblivion. If not, still the Parables did not exercise the influence on the believing and thinking of the Apostles that the Parables should have had, since they had been given by Jesus.

The Apostles, and with them the Evangelists, made a choice out of all they knew about Jesus. This choice cannot have been easy since much information was not consistent. For example, some early Christians believed in the Ascension of Jesus into Heaven straight from the Cross. "Today shalt thou be with me in paradise" (Luke 23:43) points in this direction.

The text of the Gospels shows that for the Apostles and Evangelists the first component of the Gospel is the one which has a sacramental character. Why this was their choice—not always, as the philosopher Immanuel Kant noted, in harmony with the complete text of the Gospels—lies outside of the scope of this book. Let it suffice to state that the book *Life of Hercules* had a lasting influence on the composition of this sacramental section, and tens of quotations from the New Testament confirm this.[2]

The second component of the Gospels is the so-called eschatological aspect of the Message of Jesus. This means, according to Albert Schweitzer, that one has to see the whole content of the Gospels in the light of an approaching end of the existing situation in the world. Oppressions would come during Jesus' being on earth and, soon after these, the Kingdom of God would come on earth. Also according to Schweitzer, Jesus had reached the insight that He should go to Jerusalem in order to die and, through His death, force the coming of the Kingdom of God on earth. (Schweitzer also noted that this Kingdom has not come.)

---

[2]A companion volume, scheduled for publication in the Fall of 1993, will provide the complete list of the direct correspondencies between Hercules and the biblical Jesus as portrayed in the Gospels.

Schweitzer's hypothesis, as an explanation for the eschatological texts, is a desperate attempt to explain the origins of Christianity and to provide an alternative to the liberal image of Jesus (Jesus portrayed by 19th and 20th century scholars as a most successful carpenter's son who developed himself into a spiritual teacher). But in his hypothesis Schweitzer overlooked that the Gospels portray Jesus not just as a prophet of the last things, but as He Who is the salvation and Who will be with those who really follow Him: "For where two or three are gathered together in my name, there am I in the midst of them" (Matt. 18:20).

The third component of the Gospels consists of the Parables. It is in the Parables—and in Parables only—that Jesus spoke to the multitude. This underlines the vast importance of the Parables.

The lack of attention that Christianity has directed toward the Parables has given the Parables a vast "negative" importance that should be stressed. This negative importance partially explains how the Parables have become the stepchildren of Christianity. The main elements of the Christian faith, as formulated in the Apostles' Creed from about the fifth century, are not mentioned, not even alluded to, in the Parables. It is obvious that only very few Parables have been admitted into the text of the Gospels. That any Parables have been mentioned at all can be explained by the generally accepted hypothesis that there were lists with sayings of Jesus circulated among the early Christian communities or churches. Thus, the Parables could not be excluded entirely.

Christian faith, even the early Christianity recorded in the Gospels, cannot help us in coming to a deeper understanding of the teachings of Jesus. Early Christianity was already deeply interested in problems related to orthodoxy and heresy, two subjects which are not even alluded to in the Parables. Also in the context of early Christianity, one should keep in mind that the Epistles do not give us any insight into the words of Jesus. The Epistles are, in fact, closest to component number one, the sacramental aspect of the Gospels. And the Gospels, scholars now know, were compiled after, and under the influence of, the Epistles. Thus, we see the importance of the discovery by Laurentius Valla (1407-1457) that the Apostles' Creed is not from the Apostles. Similarly, it is interesting to note that neither the Nicean Creed (325 A.D.) nor the Apostles' Creed (5th century A.D.) contains any reference to any saying of Jesus.

In the light of all this, we can conclude that a religion which is really interested in the Parables has yet to come. Later in this book we will see why we can believe that this will happen, and how such a religion might come about.

# II.

Are the Parables authentic? It is the right question to ask, but as is the case with so many of our vital and proper questions, it is difficult, if not impossible, to answer. There is one subtle indication that practically all of the Parables, in so far as they are mentioned in the Gospels, are authentic: The Parables do not fit in the framework of the Gospels. The Parables have no connection with the sacramental and eschatological components previously mentioned. In the Christian faith there is no need for the Parables since, according to the Christian faith, salvation is obtained through participating in sacraments and through believing in certain interpretations of the Cross, the Resurrection, and the Ascension into Heaven.

According to the Parables, however, salvation is obtained in a very different way. Sacramental requirements are not ever mentioned, nor is any believing requirement. The text of the Parables should have made the development of the Christian faith in a sacramental direction impossible.

The Parables themselves make it understandable to us that Christianity did, and does, leave them aside. Did not Jesus speak to the multitude in Parable only? Did Jesus not give His explanation to the disciples only (Mark 4:34) and not to the multitude? Did not, therefore, Jesus speak to the multitude in order not to be understood? This cannot have made the Parables attractive and popular.

Precisely because they have been neglected to such extent, the Parables have come to us more or less uninfluenced by the faith of the early Christians. We realize this when we become aware that St. Justin Martyr (about 150 A.D.) believed that Jesus spoke to the multitude *after* His Resurrection, whereas according to the Gospels Jesus had given His doctrine before His crucifixion. The situation of early Christianity is difficult to fathom. St. Justin Martyr did not know our Gospels. His many Gospel quotations are from an older Gospel, which we do not have.

This persistent leaving aside the words of Jesus was in a certain sense unavoidable. For example, the Parables give no justification for the existence of a cornerstone of Christianity, the doctrine of original sin. Christianity could have realized that the idea of original sin is incompatible with the words of Jesus: "Be ye therefore perfect even as your Father which is in heaven is perfect" (Matt. 5:48). Why has it not been supposed that by coming closer to the Exalted Presence of God we become more perfect?

The Parables speak to us about the eternity of God. It could be this which makes the Parables a mystery, the depth of which is indicated in Matthew 13:35: "I will open my mouth in parables. I will utter things which have been kept secret from the foundation of the world."

Bible scholars of the 20th century are confused with texts like Mark 4:34 which indicates that Jesus spoke in Parables only ("But without a parable spake he not unto them..."). Modern minds prefer another method of teaching and learning: just give them the facts. Why should the mystery of the Kingdom of God have been given, as indicated in

Mark 4:11, to the twelve only? ("And he said unto them, Unto you is given to know the mystery of the kingdom of God: but unto them that are without, all these things are done in parables.")

The reasons for this are mentioned in Matthew 13:12-13:

> For whosoever hath, to him shall be given, and he shall have more abundance: but whosoever hath not, from him shall be taken away even that he hath.
> Therefore I speak to them in parables: because they seeing see not; and hearing they hear not, neither do they understand.

in Mark 4:12

> That seeing they may see, and not perceive; and hearing they may hear, and not understand; lest at any time they should be converted, and their sins should be forgiven them.

and in Luke 8:10

> And he said, Unto you it is given to know the mysteries of the kingdom of God: but to others in parables; that seeing they might not see, and hearing they might not understand.

These verses have not been accepted as self-explanatory. The Theological Dictionary on the New Testament (Gerhard Kittel) calls the word "mystery" in Mark 4:11 a "dark" word. A dark word? Because this mystery astonishes us and makes understanding this Gospel more difficult?

One must realize that over the whole Gospel of Mark there is a mysterious haze. There a reader finds that nothing about Jesus and His teachings is easily accessible. It is interesting that in early Christianity it was generally accepted that Jesus had a different attitude in his teaching when He spoke to the inner circle than when He spoke to the multitude. In church circles it was accepted that this distinction between teaching to the few and teaching to the multitude was very far reaching.

Such an understanding in very early Christianity is important because teaching was the most important function when Jesus appeared before the multitude. Thus, leaving aside the Parables—so much so that they do not have any role in the Christian doctrine about Jesus Christ—cannot be justified. Had Christianity tried to follow Jesus as He indicated with precision and as He taught in His Parables, we would have a greater Christianity than we have today.

Therefore whosoever heareth these sayings of mine, and doeth them, I will liken him unto a wise man, which built his house upon rock:

And the rain descended, and the floods came, and the winds blew, and beat upon that house; and it fell not: for it was founded upon a rock.

And every one who heareth these sayings of mine, and doeth them not, shall be likened unto a foolish man, which built his house upon the sand:

And the rain descended, and the floods came, and the winds blew, and beat upon that house; and it fell: and great was the fall of it.

(Matt. 7:24-27)

Is it possible to explain the Parables? Verses such as Mark 4:11 ("Unto you is given to know the mystery of the kingdom of God...") and Mark 4:34 ("...and when they were alone, he expounded all things to his disciples") raise this question. The few explanations of Jesus to His disciples that we have in our Gospels do not cover the Parables in question completely, and scholars like Gerhard Kittel and Rudolf Bultmann tell us that "mystery" in Mark 4:11 is a "dark" word. They maintain that the above-quoted verses show a misunderstanding of the Parables on the part of Mark.

Nor do other parts of the Gospels help us decipher the mystery of the Parables, particularly when we would agree with the generally accepted, present-day view of scholars on the Gospels. What is this generally accepted view? In his very important and noble book *Gisteren, vandaag en morgen* (Yesterday, Today and Tomorrow), Prof. Dr. W. H. van de Pol says: "All Bible-research scholars agree that the Gospels are not historiography in the customary sense of the word; the Gospels are not biographies. They rather are testimonies of the faith of the first and second generations of Christians. They give more a historically ascertained picture of the faith of the oldest Christian congregations than of the words and acts of Jesus." (*Gisteren, vandaag en morgen* (Yesterday, Today and Tomorrow), W. H. van de Pol, Gooi en Sticht bv, Hilversum, Netherlands, 1979, p. 67) (translation by author)

The Parables in no way reflect the faith of early Christians or the early Christian orthodoxy as reflected in the sacramental and eschatological components that comprise the rest of the Gospels. Since they do not, for that very reason, the Parables are authentic. In the Parables we get a historically reliable testimony of the words of Jesus.

Apparently the early Christians must have realized that the Parables were authentic. How otherwise could the early Christians have accepted in their growing New Testament words of Jesus which did not contain anything of beliefs—not from Jesus—which were dear to the early Church?

We can surmise another reason for this acceptance of the Parables by the early Christians, but it is a reason difficult to accept as long as one operates with the presupposition that Parables can only be understood if we know their historical background. Rudolf Bultmann, for instance, says that to understand the Parables one has to know the historical situation and also the reason why Jesus gave a Parable. These, according to the Bultmann, are not known to us. According to Bultmann, Parables would become more understandable if we were better informed about the situation in Palestine at the time Jesus was on earth.

But Parables do not refer to any particular historical context. On the contrary, the examples used in the Parables are taken from everyday life—life as it had been, still is, and will be as long as there are human beings. People will marry, they will have property, and so on. The presupposition of Bultmann, and others, is so typical of a modern, secularized way of thinking.

Why not suppose that the Parables, which indeed do have a background, have their background in God's eternity? After all, Parables speak about the Kingdom of God. When one is in search for their background, why not give serious consideration to Matthew 13:35? "I will open my mouth in parables; I will utter things which have been kept secret from the foundation of the world."

In the light of this text, the mystery mentioned in Mark 4:11 becomes more understandable, paradoxical as it seems to be. Mark 4:11 and Mark 4:33-34 remind us of what Jesus had said about casting pearls before swine (Matt. 7:6). This contrasts Bultmann's attempt to link the Parables of Jesus with the historical situation of that time. The Gospels do not provide this link. Remember, the Gospels are primarily statements of faith of the first and second generations of the early Christians, not a biography.

All of this means that Jesus Christ has not founded Christianity, but Christianity has gradually formed the image of Jesus Christ. To understand that leads one towards a complete lack of clarity with regard to our knowledge regarding Jesus.

How can we resolve this lack of clarity? Here again, the importance of the Parables must be noticed. In the Parables we have the authentic words of Jesus. It is through these words that we may get an idea of what Jesus wanted us to do and, most importantly, Who Jesus is. One may well ask what course Christianity would have taken had it permitted itself to be influenced and guided by the Parables.

The Christian faith—one has only to look at the Apostles' Creed for an example—consists of a set of beliefs that were constructed by making use of selections from the New Testament. As has been pointed out, the Parables have not been used in this process of selecting texts to construct

Christianity. The Parables do not lend themselves to this kind of procedure. Why is that so?

To begin with, selecting between essentials and matters of secondary importance is only possible on the basis of full understanding. With Parables, we may well question ourselves (keeping in mind Mark 4:11) whether we do have such an understanding. To assume that we have such understanding would be nothing more than a presupposition, one which cannot be proven. Neither can we suppose that there are any extraneous details in the Parables. Every particle of a Parable has an essential function within the Parable, just as a wheel in a watch. Finally, and perhaps most importantly, would it not be presumptuous to make selections and distinctions regarding the teachings of Jesus where Jesus has given His Parables as a whole? He called His teachings a mystery, and this mystery (Mark 4:11) is the reason His teachings were given in Parables.

Even had Jesus not said it, His Parables still must have been a mystery to His audiences—and this from the "negative" point of view mentioned previously. What do the Parables not say? His audience believed in the necessity of having a temple; they believed in the Mosaic Law; they believed in the necessity of having priests and scribes; they believed in the necessity of believing certain things. Of all this, there is nothing in the Parables. That can only mean that these things were not essential in relation to the Kingdom of God.

This created a problem for early Christianity, which was already interested in a certain number of things, none of which were mentioned, or hinted at, in the Parables. One can only conclude that when Jesus spoke to the multitude there was no linkage between what Jesus taught and what the multitude believed, a situation which has not changed since. His Parables have remained a mystery.

The teachings of Jesus consist of Parables only, and "unto them that are without, all these things are done in parables." It is obvious that these words of Jesus are not and cannot be in harmony with the sacramental and eschatological components that were later included in the compilation of the Gospels. These Parables of Jesus are not only stories which teach us. Later in this book we will consider how the Parables also effectuate something, in the sense of Psalm 33:9: "For he spake and it was done; he commanded and it stood fast." This points to a conclusion: that in Mark 4:11 Jesus is revealing His relationship with God the Father, and that relationship is the sacred mystery.

The reactions towards this mystery-character of the Parables have invariably remained the same through the ages: an attitude of neglect, not-understanding, and rejection. The mystery about which Jesus speaks is not related to any kind of ritual. In fact no ritual can give any understanding of the Parables. From its beginning, however, Christianity was a ritualistic religion. This may help explain why so few Parables, out of the many there must have been, were inserted into the Gospels. Our Gospels date from about 200 A.D., and by that time Christianity had already an elaborate ritual for its church services. It was in this ritual, and not in the Parables, that Christians were looking for mystery.

But it is not only dogmatic Christianity that has shown little or no use for the mystery-character of the Parables.

Albert Schweitzer tries to explain away their implication and their application by not respecting Mark 4:34, where it is said that Jesus never did speak to the multitude other than in Parables. Schweitzer waters it down by saying "sometimes" Jesus spoke in Parables. Since the word "sometimes" does not appear in the text, Schweitzer's explanation is without foundation. His attitude, which is typical in much modern thinking, simply ignores that which does not fit into his already-existing convictions. Such attitudes have not contributed to any realization of the importance of the Parables or to any understanding of their content.

The Parables and their mystery should have been—and should be—accepted as incentives, inroads for better understanding of what Jesus has to say to all and each of us. Should we not like to know at least something about what is done (Mark 4:11) in Parables and what those things are that have been kept secret from the foundation of the world (Matt. 13:35)? It is in the Parables that Jesus guides the one who is in search of their meaning towards deeper understanding.

# III.

Why is everything about which the Parables speak expressed in such a symbolic way? Why is not everything expressed in clear terms, in clear ideas, in clear concepts, as we like to hear our preachers speak about things external? The question is whether man can be addressed in clear terms; the history of Christianity shows that it is doubtful what all these clear and precise doctrinal definitions have effectuated. What does become immediately clear when one reads the Parables is that what Jesus says about the Kingdom of God can be said in terms, symbols and images derived from everyday life.

In an earlier section, it was emphasized how it is not given to man to really explain a single Parable, to come with an understanding and insight which reveal the real meaning of each statement in the Parable and its links with the other statements in the Parable. This becomes evident when one begins to read the Parable of the Seed Growing Secretly, mentioned in Mark 4:26-29. Jesus is going to tell His hearers what the Kingdom of God is like.

> And he said, So is the kingdom of God, as if a man should cast seed into the ground;
> And should sleep, and rise night and day, and the seed should spring and grow up, he knoweth not how.

For the earth bringeth forth fruit of herself; first
the blade, then the ear, after that the full corn in the
ear.
But when the fruit is brought forth, immediately
he putteth in the sickle, because the harvest is come.


Who of us could ever think that it is in our power to
elucidate the words of Jesus? Only a few respectful remarks,
and nothing more than that, can be made.

This kingdom, being the Kingdom of God, has of course
a King. The King, God, is not mentioned: God, being the
Almighty God, is the source and origin of this kingdom;
everything comes from Him and depends on Him. Therefore
the reader realizes that what is going to come in this Parable
is only possible because of God having ordained it this way.
The Parable does not mention any general or particular
world situation; what light could that throw on sowing seed,
this being something of all times and all places? But it is
obvious that the hearers of Jesus must have been surprised:
instead of speaking about things divine in terms they were
accustomed to, Jesus compares the Kingdom of God, which
is eternal, with a man—about the last comparison they would
have expected. And what they got—and thereby what we
get—to hear about this man has no link at all with the
standards we use for assessing each other and ourselves.
Apparently this man, by doing what he did, is not only an
essential element in the Kingdom of God, but he also reflects
the fulfillment of God's will.

It may be said that if man becomes aware of the essential
role he can have in the Kingdom of God, which kingdom of
course is unlimited in time and space, the world, where man

is for a rather short while, would have for him a different aspect. In the Parable the link between the Kingdom of God and the man is there, and the man's attention is focused on it. One would expect that the man would do something exceptional, and one can suppose that such a thing is what Jesus' listeners expected to hear. Just because of the seeming contrast between the Kingdom of God on the one side and a man on the other side, Jesus has made it possible for those who heard Him to realize that behind this story the Message of God is given. The Kingdom of God is like a man who cast seed; so this kingdom is not compared with a man as such but with a man who takes a well-defined initiative, casting seed into the ground. Because the Parable tells us how this man is eagerly waiting for harvest-time, one may conclude that the ground had been prepared for making this casting of the seed meaningful and successful. It seems almost superfluous to point out the fact that in order to bring the man, the seed, and the ground into a meaningful relationship, the action of the man is needed. Everyone would agree to this. But how many of Jesus' hearers, and how many of us, follow up what Jesus said? How many realize that it is such an *action* of man with which the Kingdom of God is compared by Jesus? After all, a Parable is a story which tells us when man's actions illustrate what the Kingdom of God is.

If the ground could mean the deepest aspect of man, his heart and his mind, who then uses his lifetime for preparing his innermost being for receiving seed, seed being the symbol of the wisdom of God, without which man cannot live? Who realizes that the wisdom of God can grow in man

and will grow in man provided the ground is made clean
from all that would not be helpful for the growing of the
seed? Was it realized, at the moment Jesus gave this Parable
to the multitude, that man has a heavenly opportunity which
makes his life what it could and should be? It is clear from
the Parable that the ground received its function and its
importance from the fact that it can receive the seed, the
wisdom of God. It is exactly in the ground, in the heart and
mind of man, where the Message of God grows. Evidently
the Parable presupposes a link between God and the deepest
aspect of man's being (recalling Genesis 1:27: "So God
created man in his own image, in the image of God created
he him; male and female created he them"). This link is lost
sight of by a worldly way of life, worldly values, worldly
goals in life. In the Parable a justification for a worldly life
cannot be found. Instead of indulging in such a way of life,
this Parable teaches us that the presence of this link can be
known. One thinks here of the profound statement of Saint
Augustine: that through our knowledge of our own
consciousness we ascend to the knowledge of God, because
deep in us something, which is divine, lives. This is so
because we are created in God's image, spirit of His Spirit,
and because, in the last resort, the Father and we are one.
Jan Luyken, a Calvinistic poet of the 17th century, said that
God revealed Himself out the depth of his (i.e., Jan
Luyken's) being. These two statements show how very
careful we must be with the deepest aspect of life. When do
we do just that? When do we realize in our everyday life that
the seed should be able to grow there, where it has been cast
into the ground? That man's deepest side could be the place

where, in the Kingdom of God, God's wisdom as the food
for man can grow is, for us, the deepest mystery and the
greatest gift of God's grace that man can conceive of. If the
Parable would not have said this, who would ever have
thought of this reality?

And while the seed is springing and growing up, the man
sleeps and rises night and day, not knowing how the seed
does grow. The growing process is not this man's work. It
is beyond his powers; yet, at the same time, the man
depends on it completely for getting life's sustenance. The
Parable tells us that the man sleeps and rises. Such a thing is
also said in the Parable of the Ten Virgins (Matt. 25); the
virgins sleep and, at the appropriate moment, they arise. The
man in this Parable is like those who listened to Jesus. Of
course he does not know and cannot know what growth is,
because it comes from God and therefore contains an aspect
of God. This man sleeps and rises. Sleeping—that is not
being aware of what is going on—prepares him for
awakening, which is becoming aware of what has taken
place. The man is awake and ready when he should be. How
many of us realize that we must live an awakened life? That
is the life in which the moment of the coming of God's gifts
will not be missed. While the man in the Parable lives a life
of the usual routine, his attention is focused on the seed and
its growing. Who of us, while living our lives on earth, are
focused on what really matters, on how our lives will
become the ground for the growing of God's wisdom in us.
Who of us, to say it in the words of the Parable of the
Unjust Steward, are aware that man's deepest aspect will

become what it should become, an everlasting habitation
(Luke 16:9)?

What does the earth do, after being prepared for the
seed, when the seed has been laid in it? What does man's
innermost being do—after being prepared for it—from the
moment the wisdom of God has been laid in it? The earth
bears fruit; it is said in such a way that the man can count on
that. The earth brings forth fruit without a visible cause or
without an origin that can be traced back or investigated. The
Parable tells us here that the most important thing which can
grow in man's innermost being is beyond his knowledge.
Since Jesus speaks in this Parable about the Kingdom of
God, the cause which makes this growth possible in us forms
part of the Kingdom of God. In this Parable, not knowing,
not understanding, does not imply not seeing. The man sees
the results of his sowing. This implies that if we sow nothing
but that which comes from God in our hearts and minds,
results will become visible and noticeable in our lives, and
the results can be and will be abundant—provided we act and
live in the same way as the man in this Parable. He used the
ground, i.e., the basis of his whole being, the way it is
meant to be used.

And when the fruit permits it—so the results permit, not
the man—the man puts in the sickle immediately. In so
doing, by not waiting a second, the man shows what his real
and thereby strongest desire is—to come closer towards God.
Towards Him alone the man really aspires. In the Kingdom
of God all worldly desires fade away, and only this one
life-giving and essential desire towards God remains. And so
the Parable teaches also what purification really is. Through

his immediately acting, the man shows that he realizes how essential for him the fruit is, his life's sustenance. Who would not maintain that man needs, before anything else, God's wisdom? When one asks what precisely this wisdom contains, the answer is that, in this Parable, no description is given of the kind of seed Jesus speaks about.

What does the man do with the harvest? It is not said in the Parable. Having this harvest, what will the man do? It is not said. Nothing is said anymore. The Parable has no end; it is a story without end but, since the Parable speaks about the Kingdom of God, how could it have an end? This illustrates that the link between God and man has no end. The Parable tells us how this link can and should be used by man so that he can live on what God has permitted to grow in him. And our desire makes this process possible and visible: every tree is known by its own fruit. The Parable, speaking about the man, tells us what the importance of man is: the ground receives its importance from the fact that it can produce a harvest from the seed, which is already there in the Kingdom of God. And so the Parable tells us what the meaning of life is when our deepest desire goes to God: the meaning that man does not let a moment go by when it is possible for him to receive a harvest of the wisdom of God. And since the Parable speaks about the Kingdom of God, it tells us how eternal life can and should begin here and now in life on earth.

# IV.

The words of Jesus made a deep impression. In His sayings Jesus taught as one having authority and not as the scribes; the people were astonished at His doctrine (Matt. 7:28-29). It is indeed still astonishing that instead of saying what we should believe and what kind of rituals we should get involved in, Jesus in the Parables speaks about everyday life. Nothing about what one must do, but everything about what one may do. Nothing about the problems of the time, no allusion to the political and social views and desires of the time. No complying with the convictions of the time. Nothing about prayers and, so it seems, nothing about God. One might feel inclined to suppose that in His Parables Jesus did not give religious instruction. But one is "warned" in a sense by Jesus when He said that the mystery of the Kingdom of God and all these things are given and are done in Parables (Mark 4:11).

The way we live has a deep influence on our thinking, our feeling, and our understanding of everything we come in contact with. Purity of heart and purity of mind are of essential value; this becomes clear as soon as we realize that life on earth is a journey towards eternity, a caravan towards eternity. Nowhere in His teachings does Jesus say that there is a rupture or split between life here and life hereafter. That is a distinction our tradition began making because of

Christian ideas regarding sin, although the idea of original sin cannot be traced back to the Parables.

Strangely enough, we still make this distinction between life here on earth and life hereafter, although we make it these days for a very different reason: because our outlook on life has become completely secularized. But why should one even suppose that life has ended when the body ceases to function? Purity of heart and purity of mind bring us closer to the understanding of how very important it is to give attention, continuously, to what pleases God and to what displeases Him. That takes a lifetime—and more.

In Jesus' words to "be perfect even as your Father, which is in heaven is perfect," no limitation in time is attached. Does the magnitude of this not allow us to see that the life of the soul goes on after the existence on earth has come to an end? Jesus spoke to the multitude, and thereby to us, in teachings which are timeless, teachings which had the same importance then as they have now, teachings which are not tied to a particular period or to a particular situation.

Because they are always true, one begins to realize that the Parables have their background in the eternity of God. The idea that not only the Parables have to be understood, but also that Jesus has to be understood in the context of the situation in Palestine of some 2,000 years ago fails to appreciate that Jesus has His origin in God and in His eternity. The form and the examples, in fact all the stories of the Parables, are from beginning to end taken from everyday life. This underlies the real importance of every day of our lives—namely that everyday life, lived in accordance with the Parables, will bring our hearts and minds closer to the

Eternal God. These stories, these Parables, effectuate in us the desire for a Godpleasing life. Do we not read in Mark 4:11 that the Parables are not words only? We are warned, in the deepest sense of the word, by Jesus that the meaning and aim of our lives are not to be found in ideas, in generalities, in abstracts, but in the way each of us lives.

In His Parables Jesus has uttered "things which have been kept secret from the foundation of the world" (Matt. 13:35). Through the Parables we come in contact with something that surpasses us by far, that cannot be measured, that cannot be mastered, that points beyond us to the goal of all of us: God. How do the Parables speak about the road towards that goal?

In the Parables, according to Matthew 13:35-36, the unpronounceable remains unpronounced, but it is nevertheless conveyed to us in terms we can understand, terms derived from everyday life. That is something which should never pass unnoticed. How completely unexpected it was that Jesus spoke about the Kingdom of God while using examples taken from everyday life. Angelus Silesius described this link as follows: "The true Son of God is Christ only, However every Christian must be the same Christ" (The Cherubinic Wanderer, V, 9; translation by author). In fact, what Angelus Silesius said points to the close link between the Kingdom of God and each individual human being. Generally speaking, man is not aware of this link. His whole upbringing, his lifestyle, his values and his goals, are all are confined to the realm of this world. Man is so deeply accustomed to his own outlook on the world that he is not aware of what is beyond this world. No wonder that our present-day civilization has ended up in materialism.

Eternal life can and should begin here and now on earth. Jesus says this when He mentions the possibility, and the necessity, of being rich toward God. This is a kind of richness which has nothing to do with laying up treasure for oneself. Jesus speaks about it in the Parable of the Rich Fool (Luke 12:13-21).

> And one of the company said unto him, Master, speak to my brother, that he divide the inheritance with me.
>
> And he said unto him, Man, who made me a judge or divider over you?
>
> And he said unto them, Take heed, and beware of covetousness: for a man's life consisteth not in the abundance of the things which he possesseth.
>
> And he spoke a parable unto them, saying, The ground of a certain rich man brought forth plentifully:
>
> And he thought within himself, saying, What shall I do, because I have no room where to bestow my fruits?
>
> And he said, This will I do: I will pull down my barns, and build greater; and there will I bestow all my fruits and my goods.
>
> And I will say to my soul, Soul, thou hast much goods laid up for many years; take thine ease, eat, drink and be merry.
>
> But God said unto him, Thou fool, this night thy soul shall be required of thee: then whose shall these things be, which thou hast provided?
>
> So is he that layeth up treasure for himself, and is not rich toward God.

The question which is addressed to Jesus is drawn from life. When inheritances have to be divided, man shows his greed, often in an unmitigated way. He does not realize how dangerous greed is, not only with regard to others, but especially to himself. Greed entails a self-centeredness, which is contrary to the goal of life.

Jesus must have made a deep impression on this man because he asked Jesus such a private question in public. The question also indicates the great importance this man attached to the inheritance. In requesting that Jesus intervene in this situation, the man should have first considered whether it was Jesus' task to accede to such a request. Jesus immediately leads this man towards the insight that man cannot and should not try to drag Jesus into situations which have nothing to do with Jesus' being on earth. Jesus brings the Message of God. And so this man, and those who were there, received an answer from which they could become, in reality, richer.

With his question, the man tried to make Jesus do what he himself had not been able to achieve. With His answer, Jesus tells him what man can achieve to the benefit of the deeper side of his life.

Speaking to the man and the company, Jesus warned that they themselves are responsible for what they do and for what they should do. With this responsibility for the right kind of life, man should not fall in the pitfalls of life on earth. One such pitfall is greed, covetousness; this pitfall exercises a great attraction and influence on man. And so Jesus said that man should go through life with open eyes, he should be vigilant, and he should keep good watch on behalf

of his soul. The Greek word for covetousness explains that
there is more to covetousness than is usually realized. Its
meanings include "unreasonable profit-making, infringement
on someone else's property," and, not the least,
"arrogance." That man becomes covetous shows that man so
very often is intoxicated by the glamour of the world, so
much so that this intoxication makes him see only himself.
Greed disturbs the harmonious acting and reacting of man,
which also leads towards a disturbing of society, as Philo (25
B.C.- 40 A.D.) noted.

The Parable of the Rich Fool tells us what happens in
one's life when the real goal of life is no longer seen. Greed
may lead towards obtaining abundance of earthly goods,
which may give the owner a feeling of safety, comfort, and
relaxation—but the soul cannot feed on it. In the Parable the
use of the word "life" warns the listener against exactly this.
The word "life" is also used as opposed to "death." For life,
something else is needed, something about which this Parable
speaks, something that shows that life is not limited to this
earth, but is extended beyond the limitations of this earth. In
the Parable Jesus says that the sustenance for eternal life can
and should be acquired during life on earth.

A certain rich man, receiving the plentiful fruits of his
ground, asks himself what to do with all these fruits. This is
a problem as he does not have sufficient storage-room. Since
these fruits come from the ground, the rich man should have
been thankful. So much could have happened which could
have destroyed, or at least have impaired, the yield of the
ground. Thankfulness, however, is missing in his
matter-of-fact reasoning. He deliberates with himself only,

and he does it very carefully; the great care which he is going to take in implementing a plan shows this. But he does not deliberate as he should have. What follows in the Parable makes this clear. From a worldly point of view, his way of handling his property makes a lot of sense. In fact, who would not have acted as the Rich Fool did? For the reader of the Parable, this Parable is a kind of a mirror. It shows how deeply man entrenches himself in ways of thinking and acting that make it impossible for him to experience precisely that which the Rich Fool was lacking—and it thus reflects the world as it is today. In the words of Angelus Silesius: "When you think of God, then you hear Him in you, Would you be silent and quiet, He would speak unceasingly" (Cherubinic Wanderer, V, 330). Man should show in his behavior that he is fully aware of the link which God has established between Him and him.

The effort which the Rich Fool is going to make for storing his fruits and his goods is substantial. It is an enterprise that will guarantee to the Rich Fool that he will be able to enjoy for a very long time the results of all his efforts. Here the Rich Fool illustrates the general lifestyle of man. Being comfortable and at home in the world has become a goal in itself. We can read what the man really thinks that his goals are; they are described with precision in what the Rich Fool says to his soul. But the four attractions that are mentioned exclude the knowing of oneself as being dependent on God and, thus, needing to direct oneself towards a life of sanctification. A man with goals in life such as those of the Rich Fool isolates himself from real life. He keeps his goods for himself. That seems wise, but when one acts that way one does not prepare oneself for the realities of life. This Parable goes on to say what these realities are.

The Rich Fool is not ready for God's speaking to him. What supports him at the moment? Not his soul, for which he intended to make all sorts of efforts, as his soul will be required of him. The Rich Fool intended to give to his soul peace and undisturbed relaxation. He thought that a state of bliss for his soul could be obtained through providing earthly goods. He really thought that his soul could live on earthly goods. When we look around at others and, above all, at ourselves, the question must arise: In what way are we different from the Rich Fool? Who wishes to realize that one's soul is one's innermost part, which has—as long as it is on earth—a continuous desire to go back to its Creator, God? Who wishes to become conscious of the fact that man, with his predominant desire for earthly goods, has no time for laying up treasures in heaven? In his speaking to his soul, the Rich Fool shows that he has no idea what he is really saving. He should have known, and he could have known, that his soul, not being his property, is his link with the Almighty God. And therefore his life should have been subservient to that awareness.

God says "fool" in addressing the man. If Jesus had not said it, we might have found it embarrassing that God would say such a thing in the Parable. This word, "fool," epitomizes God's displeasure. At the very same moment, it opens the road towards the real goal of life. The word "fool" shows how very empty-handed man is when he has only collected the things he has to leave behind on this earth. This word is a ringing warning that laying up these kinds treasures for oneself ends up in foolishness.

"This night thy soul shall be required of thee." This soul's time for being on earth is coming to an end, soon, this night. The Parable does not tell us what happened to the Rich Fool between the moment God spoke to him and the moment his soul was actually required of him. What takes place between God and the soul of each of us is not meant to be known by anybody else. Nor does the Parable tell us what happened to the soul of the Rich Fool after it was required of him. This also is beyond our comprehension and our judgment. It is not meant to be known by anybody else. But we may say that the serious consequences of our way of life here on earth cannot be stressed in a more forceful way than is done in this Parable.

Jesus does not let the Parable end there. Jesus tells His listeners, and thereby us, that one can do something to avoid having the attitude of the Rich Fool—and one must do it. In a sense, everything preceding the very last words of Jesus in this Parable underlines the immense importance of the statement that we find in the last verse.

Man is not a fool when he becomes rich toward God. For such a man the intoxication of the world is not a temptation. A man who, through his endeavor, becomes rich toward God knows that God speaks to all and each of us: "When you think of God, then you hear Him in you, Would you be silent and quiet, He would speak unceasingly" (Cherubinic Wanderer, V, 330).

Did Jesus say what it is to be rich toward God? Jesus made it clear that man has to be in search of this being rich, a richness which has true value in the eyes of God, a richness which has nothing in common with covetousness. This aspect of the Message of Jesus is so very deep—being something which goes toward God—that it cannot be said in human words, although it can, nevertheless, be done by man. It may also mean that this richness is not something man can ever show to others. The words of Jesus stress that God is the only One where one can become really rich.

In this regard, the Parable speaks not about being rich "in" God, but about being rich "toward" God. Because God has no end, does the word "toward" not also mean that God's goodness, whereby He permits us to be rich in Him, is endless? Does not, therefore, the word "toward" reveal to us an aspect of God? Does this word not also tell us that man can be rich toward God as long as man lives?

With this Parable, Jesus brings those who listen to Him close into the exalted presence of God. And so in this Parable Jesus tells us what the reality of life, of our existence, is. How do we prevent ourselves from ever coming into the situation of the Rich Fool, who had only himself and who listened to himself only? How do we make it possible that we will avoid a lifestyle whereby we become the victims of our own greed? How can we prevent becoming a fool in the eyes of God? How do we acquire that steadfastness which is needed for the kind of life Jesus is speaking about in this Parable? How can we become rich toward God?

Angelus Silesius said: "He who lives with a pure heart and goes on the path of Christ, He adores God in an essential way within himself" (Cherubinic Wanderer, I, 238).

# V.

If man looks to accepted values for guides to proper believing and proper behaving, he will mislead himself. When Jesus spoke to the multitude, it was clear that no accepted view of that time could be a vehicle for deeper understanding. Jesus made that clear through His own attitude with regard to the religious and social convictions of that time. That attitude has not lost anything of its importance and its actuality because current-day Christianity is not yet substantially different from conventional Jewish life of 2,000 years ago. The way we should live—as exemplified in the Parables, the Sermon on the Mount, and, specifically, the Beatitudes—has been lived by Jesus, not by His followers. This was made clear in a far-reaching, important, and noble analysis given by Prof. Dr. W. H. van de Pol:

"Had Jesus not completely unnecessarily (i.e., from the point of view of the Pharisees, the Sadducees, the priest and the scribes) undermined the prestige of the priest and the Levitate through His Parable of the Good Samaritan? Had Jesus through His preaching not undermined the authority over the population which Pharisees and scribes enjoyed? Had Jesus not in all sorts of ways transgressed the Law of Moses by healing the sick on the Sabbath, by not fasting and by not keeping the customary ablutions? Was it not simply a slap in the face of the holy Law, that Jesus did eat and drink with public sinners and the despised Publicans, who exploited the population for the benefit of the Romans; that He took under His protection a prostitute caught in the act of

her profession; that He nota bene let such a suspected
woman kiss His feet in the presence of His host and his
guests? Did Jesus not endanger the whole social order
through His criticism of the rich and by encouraging them
not to invite to their dish their peers but the poor and the
homeless, i.e. the scum of society? Was it not in
contravention to every kind of convention, that Jesus did
associate amicably with women and with Samaritans? Were
the grievances of the leaders of the population not in every
respect legitimate and well-founded?

What on the other hand did Jesus mean when He said:
"Judge not, that ye be not judged. For with what judgment
ye judge, ye shall be judged: and with what measure ye
mete, it shall be measured to you again" (Matt. 7:1-2). Is it
perhaps because neither do we really know someone else's
heart nor our own heart? Is it perhaps because all of us are
sinners and do need God's forgiveness, and that therefore
only God and not one single human being has the right to
judge? Has Jesus ever urged His disciples to especially
condemn every one who acts wrongly? Or has Jesus asked
from His followers that at all times they should forgive until
seventy times seven (Matt. 18:22) every evil, also when that
evil would have been committed against themselves?

Has it not been a purpose of Jesus to educate His
disciples and His followers towards a radically new attitude
towards one's fellow-man, towards a life in accordance with
the spirit and not just with the letter of the law, in a word
towards a life not based on right but on love? Did Jesus in
the Parable of the Lost Son take sides with the elder son,
who for many years had served his father faithfully and

obediently? Has Jesus not rather taken sides with the younger son, who—after having become wise through adversity—had come back to his parental home and had Jesus thereby not taken sides against the (one would say) fully justified reproach of the elder son, meant for his father?

In a word: has Jesus not said explicitly—"For I say unto you, That except your righteousness shall exceed the righteousness of the scribes and the Pharisees, ye shall in no case enter into the kingdom of heaven" (Matt. 5:20). Has it not been Jesus' intention to say, with these words, that the attitude of the Christian towards his fellow-man should be of a totally different, new and higher order than that of the current morality of conventional Jewry?

Now the question is: can we in all sincerity maintain that the radical change of all standards with regard to human relations, which is the nucleus of the preaching of Jesus, in fact has found its expression and its application in the current civil morality of conventional Christianity? Or should we have to say that the great seriousness with which conventional Christianity has tried to bring its faith into line with the testimony of the Bible has been inversely proportional to the trifling earnestness with which conventional Christianity has been striving after a way of life and after an attitude in life as Jesus meant us to have? When one investigates the nature and the content of the morality of conventional Christianity, then one will have to come to the conclusion that this morality has not distinguished itself in any aspect whatsoever from that of the Jews and the gentiles." (*Gisteren, Vandaag en Morgen* (Yesterday, Today and Tomorrow), W. H. van de Pol, Gooi en Sticht bv

Hilversum, Netherlands, 1979, pp. 43-44) (translation by author)

It is obvious, from the text of the Gospels in general and from the Parables in particular, that Jesus lived and acted differently from the ways of conventional religion. It is also clear from the Parables that Jesus has not founded a new society on earth with its purpose in itself. Jesus spoke about the way of living we should adopt as a preparation for eternity. As a result, this the earth could become, and should become, what the Parables and the Sermon on the Mount indicate. In our secularized time, man tries to improve the earth without giving a thought to eternal life with God. Is this the reason why our present society is what it is? In His Parables, Jesus nowhere refers to a particular situation existing at the time when Jesus was on earth; these situations did not point towards eternity. What does?

We find that we are directed to an answer by the Gospel of Mark. There we read that the Parables speak about a mystery and they themselves are this mystery at the same time (Mark 4:11). How can we come closer to this mystery? By trusting our lives, our existence, to what we read in Mark 12:33, to love God "with all the heart, and with all the understanding, and with all the soul, and with all the strength, and to love his neighbor as himself, is more than all whole burnt offerings and sacrifices." The result, beyond our limited understanding and limited experiences, is indicated in Jesus' response to the scribe in Mark. 12:34: "And when Jesus saw that he answered discreetly, he said unto him, Thou art not far from the kingdom of God." One would think that what the scribe said (in verse 33) would have been commonly realized, although he speaks about a mystery; but what he said goes right against conventional religion. Jesus told him how essential it is to get away from the concepts and convictions of conventional religion. With His "I say unto you" Jesus made a stand against what man thinks has meaning and value for eternity. Jesus placed His "I say unto you" against the Law, the Temple, and the priesthood. Those things are not mentioned in the Parables, and the Parables collectively form the instruction for the multitude, for mankind.

Jesus brought before the multitude a reality which most had not even suspected.

> For I say to you, That except your righteousness shall exceed the righteousness of the scribes and Pharisees, ye shall in no case enter into the kingdom of heaven.
> Ye have heard it that it was said by them of old time, Thou shalt not kill; and whosover shall kill shall be in danger of the judgment:
> But I say unto you, That whosover is angry at his brother without a cause shall be in danger of the judgment...          (Matt. 5:20-22)

> Be ye therefore perfect, even as your Father which is in heaven is perfect.
>                     (Matt. 5:48)

This new reality so deeply impressed the multitude they became astonished (Matt. 7:28). And it is exactly the words of Jesus which lead us to the ultimate truth when we listen, as the scribe in Mark 12 did, to Jesus.

The teachings of Jesus speak constantly about the close link between God and man, and we begin to realize a little bit more, step by step, why it could be that Jesus gives us in the Parables examples derived from the everyday life of man. In His teachings—and that is so very attractive for us—we do not come in contact with the powers of the world nor with organized religions and their problems. The walls which man has constructed between God and man are not there in the Parables. One of the consequences of this is that the prerequisites which must be accepted for admission into any kind of organized religion are never mentioned. Everyone can do what is said in the Parables. No one needs to be restricted from entering in. What one has to do we see, as the scribe did, in Mark 12:29-34. But that is not a prerequisite, that is religion itself. That is the desire to have an open heart and an open mind for the teachings of Jesus. It is a life-long process because what Jesus says about life is not restricted by age.

The instruction of Jesus speaks of growth. Of what? And where is the end? The distinction between time and eternity is not mentioned in the Parables. That leads us towards Matthew 5:48 and a realization that this process of growth can go on until we are perfect, even as our Father which is in heaven is perfect. Therefore the Parables are not sources of information which we can understand, assess, and thereby look beyond. That would mean that we could judge them. No, what the Parables tell us makes us realize that, in order to understand something of the Kingdom of God, acting in the ways exemplified in each Parable is indispensable. Being perfect implies also our thinking, our attitude towards all which surrounds us—all of which, Schweitzer noted, is mystery. In one way or another, man is involved on the way towards becoming perfect. Along this way one sees that each Parable provides the reader with a key to further understanding of the Kingdom of God. In His teachings Jesus spoke as One having authority and not as the scribes (Matt. 7:29); the people, accustomed to listening to the scribes, were astonished at His doctrine.

It has been tried, again and again, to prove that the teachings of Jesus in the Sermon on the Mount and in the Parables were not that different from those of the scribes and the rabbis of the time when Jesus was on earth. But a close look will prove that with regard to cult, ceremonies, purity, the ban and swearing, marriage, the Great Commandment, tradition, love and forgiveness, etc., the teachings of Jesus are different from what people had then—and have to this day—been given by their religious leaders. In the way Jesus pronounced His Parables, His authority took the place of all the human burnt offerings and sacrifices, i.e., ceremonies which had obscured an understanding of how to love God and one's neighbor. In the Parables there is no reference to any of the conventional ceremonies. In fact, the burnt offerings and sacrifices are less than loving God and loving one's neighbor.

# VI.

Does the Parable of the Unjust Steward (Luke 16:1-15) tell man how to live? For ages, Christianity has been embarrassed with this Parable, and it has not known what to think of a Parable which seems to advocate dishonesty.

And he said also unto his disciples, There was a certain rich man, which had a steward; and the same was accused unto him that he had wasted his goods.

And he called him, and said unto him, How is it that I hear this of thee? give an account of thy stewardship; for thou mayest be no longer steward.

Then the steward said within himself, What shall I do for my lord taketh away from me the stewardship: I cannot dig; to beg I am ashamed.

I am resolved what to do, that, when I am put out of the stewardship, they may receive me into their houses.

So he called every one of his lord's debtors unto him, and said unto the first, How much owest thou unto my lord?

And he said, An hundred measures of oil. And he said unto him, Take thy bill, and sit down quickly, and write fifty.

Then said he to another, And how much owest thou? And he said, An hundred measures of wheat. And he said unto him, Take thy bill, and write fourscore.

And the lord commended the unjust steward, because he had done wisely: for the children of this

world are in their generation wiser than the children
of light.

And I say unto you, Make to yourselves friends of
the mammon of unrighteousness; that, when ye fail,
they may receive you into everlasting habitations.

He that is faithful in that which is least is faithful
also in much: and he that is unjust in the least is
unjust also in much.

If therefore ye have not been faithful in the
unrighteous mammon, who will commit to your trust
the true riches?

And if ye have not been faithful in that which is
another man's, who shall give you that which is
your own?

No servant can serve two masters: for either he
will hate the one, and love the other; or else he will
hold to the one, and despise the other. Ye cannot
serve God and mammon.

And the Pharisees also, who were covetous, heard
all these things: and they derided him.

And he said unto them, Ye are they which justify
yourselves before man; but God knoweth your
hearts: for that which is highly esteemed among men
is abomination in the sight of God.


We can safely assume that Jesus was aware of possible
unkind reactions, in case His audience would understand the
Parable in a literal way, towards His mentioning of doing
business. But this Parable should not be understood in a
literal way because we know that Jesus spoke only about
eternal life with God, and this in examples derived from
everyday life. It is only a literal understanding which makes
this Parable absurd, and it is precisely this absurdity which
forces the reader to ask what Jesus really is conveying to

him. The form of this Parable seems to stem from worldly wisdom; the content, however, brings the wisdom of eternal life. The Pharisees, being covetous, did not understand this Parable; this is known because they derided Jesus. The gospel does not mention anything about the reactions of the other listeners, which included His disciples.

While speaking about eternal life, this Parable therefore speaks about the importance of how we do business on earth, particularly because doing business brings man in contact with his fellow man. It is so very remarkable that the road towards the Kingdom of Heaven is traced by referring to doing business—and what is more earthly than doing business? In going on this road, man reaches the goal of life. The road to God begins here on earth, a most inspiring and uplifting message of this Parable.

Right at the beginning of the Parable, Jesus speaks about Him who is the center of this Parable, God. Jesus speaks about God in the vaguest possible way, "a certain rich man." There are so many rich men; so who is this one? In religion, when one speaks about a rich man, there is only One Who is the owner of all there is and all that exists: God. And what follows in the Parable confirms this. What the rich man did had nothing in common with earthly behavior. What the rich man said about His steward does not fit what generally was, and is, thought and said about God. This Parable could not be pleasing to the Pharisees, and their deriding Jesus confirms this.

When one compares this with other Parables, it becomes clear that Jesus spoke about eternity in an unusual and therefore unexpected way. By doing it this way, Jesus teaches His listeners, and His readers, that God is so very different from what man thinks God is—and also that God deals with man in unusual and therefore unexpected ways.

Suppose that there may have been some doubt about whom Jesus was speaking. The ensuing content of this Parable must have removed this doubt. Also, the Parable must have been considered to be of the utmost importance since, the gospel notes, Jesus gave it "also unto His disciples," who were prepared by Jesus for bring ₙHis *ing* message to the world. The Pharisees also heard all these things, but how could they have had any appreciation for these sayings of Jesus since they held in high esteem that which is abomination in the sight of God?

The rich man, being God, has a steward. From the opening words of this Parable, Jesus let His listeners realize that the Kingdom of God is different from what man thinks it is. Having a steward is an important aspect of the Kingdom of Heaven since Jesus mentions the same situation in the Parable of the Laborers in the Vineyard, in which the lord of the vineyard has a steward (Matt. 20:8). To have a steward is a normal procedure on earth; but with God? Who could it be, someone who would have the trust and confidence of God? If Jesus' listeners knew the book of Job, they would have known that God had complete confidence in Job. Who then is this steward? Every person is God's steward because man has received something in his heart from God. That something which man has received remains God's—the word steward underlines this—but it is something which man has to administer. As John Calvin noted, experience testifies to it, that the seed of religion is laid in each and all of us.

This gift from God cannot be properly administered when man gets entangled in the values of this world. When that happens, the situation, described in this Parable as having wasted the goods of His Master, sets in. For this the steward is accused unto God. The Parable does not say who accused the steward.

At this point it should be noted that the translation of the Greek work "oikonomos" as "steward" does not do complete justice to the meaning of this Greek word. The basic meaning is: he who is in charge of the house. In the Parable this word thus suggests a closer link between the rich man and the steward than would be the case with a steward who did not live in the house of the rich man. It is the rich man who not only made the appointment, but who also wanted the steward to be close to him while the steward was to keep the house in good order. The decisive importance of this is immediately seen when one realizes that in symbolic language the word "house" means the human heart. The word "house" has such an important place in this Parable.

In the first verse of the Parable, Jesus has immediately made clear the position of each individual being in relationship to God. What follows in the Parable makes it evident that, regardless of this closeness, each man has his responsibilities and—what we might not expect—his freedom in making decisions. The steward made the wrong decisions. It may be supposed that the accusations came from others who worked in the house. Jesus speaks about life with God, and it should be noted that living a religious life makes one sensitive to what goes on in the hearts and minds of those one comes in contact with. All this is made difficult to understand in our present-day world because man considers himself to be an independent being, forgetting that he is an intendant of God.

The Parable makes clear, right from the start, that God gives attention to such accusations. The Parable also makes clear from the start that the kingdom of heaven is very different from what man often thinks it is. And so the unjust steward is called, and the rich man gives the unjust steward an opportunity to justify his actions. That is the only thing the Parable at this juncture says about the rich man: that He called the unjust steward to account. No judgment is mentioned. And so the unjust steward gets time and opportunity to rectify his relationship with his Master, which is necessary if he wishes to remain a steward of God. Without getting any information about what the rich man may have thought or done, the reader later learns that the rich man, the Lord, praised the unjust steward. All this reminds the reader of the book of Job, in which God gives Job the possibility to prove that he (Job) will never cease to trust God. In this Parable the rich man gives His steward the possibility to do what the steward really wanted to do: to find his way back towards the rich man, God.

The reaction of the unjust steward to the summons makes clear that he had indeed wasted the goods of his Master and that he fully realized the implications. Why then had he done this? This the Parable does not say. However, one may suppose that through his contact with life on earth the steward had become world-like, materialistic, and that makes one lose the finer and higher aspect of life. When one loses sight of the goal of life, God, then the world becomes of overriding importance.

"What shall I do?" The steward realizes the seriousness of his situation. What is left to man when he can be no longer a steward? This Parable confirms what Angelus Silesius said: God does not punish the sinners, their own anxieties punish them (Cherubinic Wanderer V, 55).

"What shall I do?" Digging is not possible for the steward. He says he cannot do that. How can he say that, since everybody can dig? It is here that the reader should remember that the Parable is given in symbolic language. Digging in symbolic language stands for digging out of oneself the deeper side of life, the relationship with God. The steward could not dig as a result of what he had done, wasting the goods of his Master. To try a second approach, to beg, the steward feels ashamed. Asking and begging would be undignified after what he had done. One may suppose that the steward realized that, in the sight of God, it is deeds—not words—which count. The steward may also have realized that in fact there is only One Who has the right to ask, and that is God.

A third way is still open, and the steward shows that he knows this. His course of action proves this. He is going to do something whereby he will be received in the houses of his lord's debtors, although by then—as he supposes—the stewardship may have been taken away from him. By doing this, the unjust steward hopes to find protection and shelter needed for his survival. To be received in their houses will certainly happen when there is a relationship of understanding, of sympathy, between these debtors and the steward. What really is the kindness which the steward intends to show? It is the kindness of the "third" way, the way of brotherhood, the way of helping, of not condemning, the way of the open heart. This way, the Parable shows, also leads to God. The "houses" will open up because of the attitude of the steward towards these debtors. In symbolic language, the houses are the hearts of men. And so the Parable indicates what the impact of brotherhood is on the hearts of men.

The steward calls all the debtors of the rich man, and he wants to know from each debtor what he owes the rich man, who is still called the steward's lord. Then the Parable takes a sudden turn, one which makes the reader realize that the question which the steward asks each debtor is a question to which each debtor—and who is not a debtor in the sight of God?—has to know the right answer. The question, "How much owest thou unto my lord?" may be understood in the context of the Parables: how far does thou—because of thy life—stand away from God? How could the unjust steward suggest to sit down quickly and write down not what the debtor knew his debt to be, but to cut that debt in half? Not a hundred measures of oil but fifty? To a debtor who owes one hundred measures of wheat, the steward does not say write down fifty, but eighty. And why does the steward only say to the first debtor sit down quickly? Why did he not say this to the second debtor?

The debt in the first case consists of a hundred measures of oil. In the second case, the debt is a hundred measures of wheat. What do these indicate? The debt is what one owes

God, represented in one hundred measures of oil and one hundred measures of wheat. One hundred means a totality. Thus all the oil and all the wheat are owed by the two debtors to God. Oil is that which keeps the heart burning, thereby radiating love and compassion. Wheat is the food needed in life for reaching life's goal; it is the wisdom of how life on earth has to be lived. The debtors know how much they owe God, and now the steward is going to diminish their debt. But how can man do this? By passing on, by giving out what lives in his own heart, the steward thereby can give fifty measures of oil. Love comes first. It is followed by wisdom, which grows gradually when it is preceded by love that makes the hearts of men melt. Love can be given by man easier and faster than wisdom; wisdom grows slowly.

What the steward gave, he had received from God. How does the Parable indicate this? By mentioning in the beginning that there was a rich man. Only God has, man has nothing, and so the steward passed on property of God. Only that which comes from God helps man in life. God commended the unjust steward because he had done wisely—about the last thing Jesus' listeners can have expected to hear. Trying to understand this Parable in a literal sense, one is forced to say what the well-known theologian Professor C. H. Dodd said, namely that this commending is palpably absurd. But this erroneous and misleading understanding should help man to realize that this Parable cannot be approached with literal explanations. Immanuel Kant, undoubtedly one of the greatest philosophers, long ago realized that the doctrine of Jesus abolishes man's accepted views on beliefs and behavior. Kant realized that man should change these beliefs and behaviors, or at least reconsider them.

The Lord commended the steward. Stealing had not taken place. On the contrary, the unjust steward had made a wise use of the gifts of God, wise because he himself and others benefitted from this use. The Lord not only praises the unjust steward, but also says why He is praising him. It is this explanation which indicates that in this Parable the rich man is God. How otherwise could the rich man know that the children of this world are in their generation wiser than the children of light?

The children of light are the angels. Can man be wiser than the angels and, if so, how can man show this? Here this Parable points out that man can do something which is unique in the phase of his existence on earth. Through his not-condemning, through his sympathy and his understanding, man can help his fellow man to find the way out of the darkness, and the density of the earth, towards God. Angelus Silesius answered the question of what mankind is in the following way:

> Do you ask what mankind is? I am ready to say to
> you in one word, it is the superangelhood.
> (Cherubinic Wanderer, II, 44)

Why then is the steward still called unjust? The fact is that in the Greek text he is not called that, but rather he is called the steward of unlawful deeds or acts. Certainly that is the way he outwardly seemed to be, but the commending of the Lord indicates that man does not have the capability to know what really takes place when a man is doing something. Unbeknownst, the steward had done wisely. He was able to act wisely for a reason that man is not generally aware: the children of this world are in their generation wiser than the children of light. Notice that the Parable not only says that man can act wisely because man is wiser than the children of light, but also adds the words "in their generation." In the Greek language, these words mean "towards their fellow men." This indicates that while on his way towards God, man has to be a help and a support to his fellow man, a message which forms the end of this Parable. Jesus, however, goes on speaking about certain implications of this Parable. It appears that Jesus does this with the authority he has, linking what He is going to say with what God had said at the end of the Parable. Jesus' listeners, accustomed as they were to teachings formulated in symbolic language, must have realized Who was meant by the rich man, and by the Lord, and so they must have been surprised—if not shocked—that Jesus links His authority with the authority of God. Such a turn in this Parable helps the reader begin to realize in Whose presence he is when he comes in contact with the words of Jesus.

Near the end of this Parable, Jesus uses words that man does not expect to hear. In the New Testament, only Jesus uses the word "mammon." The word "mammon" not only means wealth, but also something in which one should never put one's trust. Knowing this, the words "mammon of unrighteousness" can mean life on earth. The adherents to life on earth are those who have been absorbed by worldly life. To make friends with those men can mean, in the light of this Parable, to give to them in the same way the unjust steward had done. He gave to them from the heart—and mind—qualities received from God. The Parable thus advises that man remain faithful to God while helping other men. Through such help, other men can shake off the intoxication of earthly life. Man can give this invaluable help without damage to himself. On the contrary! He who passes on these gifts knows that he has his background in God's eternity. This Parable makes clear that the world exercises a great attraction on mankind in countless ways. Therefore everyone needs the help and the support of those who show sympathy and give wisdom. And when a man, in his turn, needs the help of those he has helped in the way the Parable has described, then he may be received in everlasting habitations, as Jesus says.

In saying this, Jesus again gives His listeners and His readers the opportunity to realize in Whose presence they are. What Jesus says is given in a magnificent image. When man awakens out of his intoxication, his heart becomes a temple of eternity, a temple of God. Eternal life is in a heart which awakens toward real adoration of God. As noted, the word house is a symbolic word for the human heart. The houses have become everlasting habitations through what the steward did. And when Jesus speaks of everlasting habitations, Jesus says that these hearts have become temples of God. In a temple of God, man will find refuge. Again, what this Parable presents is magnificent. It conveys the message that the heart of man can be eternal.

It should be mentioned that the Authorized Version gives a translation (verse 9) which is not accurate enough. The Greek text does not speak of everlasting habitations, but of "the" everlasting habitations. The article indicates that Jesus is not speaking metaphorically, but that He is speaking about habitations, houses, which form part of eternity. Here the Greek word for habitation has the connotation of being related with God. These habitations, since they are eternal, are the abode of God. This, in a profound way speaks, about God's omnipresence. The Greek word for habitation also indicates that this habitation gives a closer and stronger habitation than the steward had wished for himself.

Jesus shows in this Parable what a most important role man can have in the kingdom of God. That role is, to say the least, cosmic. And it is in this life here on earth where man has the opportunity to fulfill this role. The Parable shows what stupendous task man can accomplish: to pass on eternity to his fellow man. It makes us realize that man apparently can acquire a potential which, in our present-day secularized era, is not even suspected.

This potential role of man in the Kingdom of God recalls a saying of Angelus Silesius:

> You have got to be extended
> Extend your heart, then God will enter it;
> You must be His kingdom of heaven, He wants
> to be your king.
>
> (Cherubinic Wanderer, II, 106)

The Parable tells us that he who is faithful in that which is least shows that he can be trusted, that he can be relied upon by those who in this life have become worldly and, therefore, who are in need. In the light of this Parable, "that which is least" is least in comparison with the rich man, God. The Parable, in a sense, describes the way through a test: when one has proven himself to be faithful, he is faithful in much. When he is faithful to men, man is faithful towards God. Again one thinks of Job, even more so since the word "faithful" in the Greek language has also the connotation of having hope in God. It is of the utmost importance that man is just in whatever he does. Jesus says that man's life should be void of injustice. The idea that injustice could be of minor importance is here dismissed. Man should be mindful of Psalm 33:14: "From the place of His habitation He looketh intently upon all the inhabitants of the earth."

Life here on earth is characterized by Jesus as the unrighteous mammon. Therefore one has to be faithful towards God in his dealings with his fellow men. Being faithful to God is, in fact, essential; without such faithfulness, who will commit to one's trust "that which is true," as the Greek text says? "That which is true" is referred to here as being in contrast to that which is not true, namely the world and its glamour. "That which is true" also in Greek means that which is an attribute of God. Jesus tells His listeners that man can be entrusted with something that not only surpasses man himself, and his understanding, but which also gives to his life the proper direction, namely to God. How could he who is not on this road to God be faithful in that which is another man's? In the light of this Parable, "that which is another man's" is his well-being.

It is the task of man in this life to help, just as the steward helped. This help should be sustained; the word faithful points in this direction. By giving this help, man himself will receive what is his own. The formulation, when taken in a literal sense, is a paradox. Nevertheless, in this Parable, that is exactly what is indicated: by passing on to man what he really needs (and what he really needs is God's), man himself receives what he should have and that which should be his own.

This recalls other words of Jesus about laying up treasures for oneself in heaven (Matt. 6:20). Here in Luke 16 the reader is made aware that man becomes fully man only when, and not a moment sooner, he behaves as is pointed out in the Parable, when he is faithful in that which is another man's. If man does not behave that way, how could he think that there would be someone who could give him what he needs?

It seems that Jesus does not explain what, exactly, it is that is one's own. But the attentive reader, who in a sense still hears Jesus speaking about oil and wheat, knows that he owes it to God to have those heart and mind qualities as part of his being. All of this points to a closeness between God and man which can become man's greatest strength in life. Angelus Silesius expressed it by saying that the knower has to become the known:

> In God nothing is known: He is an unique being,
> What one knows in Him, that one has to be oneself.
> (Cherubinic Wanderer, I, 285)

In the Parable, Jesus warns His listeners. Man generally attempts to serve more than one master, but even a slave cannot truly serve two masters because he will be led by his feelings. Man cannot serve mammon if he wants to serve God. A clear distinction is made here between making oneself a friend of the mammon and, on the other hand, serving mammon. Again Jesus warns with final authority and tells His listeners how eminently dangerous money is. Society would now be very different had the warning of Jesus become part of the Christian message. Never should man come in the grip of earthly riches.  When man is covetous, he is laying up treasures upon earth. What that means, Jesus has made that absolutely clear: "For where your treasure is, there will your heart be also" (Matt. 6:21). Not only His disciples, but also the Pharisees heard what Jesus had said. Being covetous, did the Pharisees really hear?

The Greek word for hearing means also: to hear something about others, to hear something about oneself. Hearing also means understanding, and this word plays an immensely important role in the Gospels. By deriding Jesus, the Pharisees showed that they had made it impossible for themselves to understand the words of Jesus. Their deriding shows a fundamental lack of respect for Jesus and His Message; it also shows how distant their hearts were from what should have been happening to their hearts. Being covetous, the Pharisees belonged to those who justified themselves before men, something which is constantly done. But Jesus says: "God knowest your heart" (recalling Psalm 33:14: "From the place of His habitation He looketh intently upon all the inhabitants of the earth").

What value then is there really in justifying oneself before men? What is highly esteemed among men is an abomination in the sight of God. The very strong word "abomination" speaks for itself, but the Greek word conveys several meanings of warning. "Abomination" is everything which is idolatrous, which makes a true relationship with God impossible. It is that which strives against God.

We may well ask, Why this sudden seriousness and severity? Because, as this Parable also says, man forms part of eternity. Angelus Silesius notes that this is true whether man wants it to be the case or not:

> To us eternity is innate
> Eternity is to us so close and forming part of us,
> Whether we will it or not, we must be eternal.
> (Cherubinic Wanderer, V, 235)

With this in mind, we begin to see that this Parable is, for each reader, a timely warning. The words of Jesus are given in order to awaken. If man awakes, his heart becomes a temple of eternity, a temple of God.

The reality, then, is as Angelus Silesius said:

> Time is nobler than eternity
> Time is nobler than a thousand eternities;
> Here I can prepare myself for the Lord,
>     there however not.
> (Cherubinic Wanderer, V, 125)

# VII.

The Parables posit a link, and all their contents have this link as their basis: the link with God and with what God has created. The basis of the Parables is that reality is one and interwoven, not an abstract idea but a reality created and sustained by God. The Parables speak about this link, thereby explaining something about it. Moreover, the Parables tell us what happens when we become aware of this link, what happens when we begin to apply it in our lives. Even to the Pharisees, Jesus has said that the Kingdom of God is within (Luke 17:21). Although the Pharisees did not realize it, the Kingdom of God is the indelible part of man. We read this also in a Gospel fragment, which is not in our Bible; there Jesus said: "The Kingdom of God is within you; he, who knows what is within him, will find it" (Oxyrrhynchos fragment).

The idea that the Kingdom of God is within us has never been an attractive idea for many Christian theologians. And this dislike has had such an impact that in Luke 17:21 many Bible translators have mistranslated the word "in" as "among". Why this rejection of Luke's intensified form of the Greek word "in"? This intensification should make any misinterpretation impossible. With regard to this text, it is very important to know that Jesus spoke not only Aramaic but also Greek. There is even speculation that the oldest

Gospel was written in Greek and later underwent an Aramaic revision. The translation "among you" is so obviously wrong because it is well known which Greek words the Gospel of Luke would have used for such an expression had Luke intended the meaning that these translators have assigned. But, nevertheless, the misinterpretation persists. This is the case because this text cannot be fitted in the basic ideas of Christian theology. This example of ignoring and wrongly translating a word of Jesus is again a warning of how essential it is, when one reads words of Jesus, not to twist what Jesus said in the direction of Christian doctrine. That is a later doctrine.

The Kingdom of God is within you, said Jesus, and the Paul echoed this in saying to the Athenians: "In God we live and move and have our being" (Acts 17:28). The essence of man is not man himself, an insight one comes across in the Parables constantly.

St. Justin Martyr made a comment which is of essential value for understanding the Parables: "For Christ is the personal form of appearance of the Word, which dwells in every man." Other early Christians believed this, and they were convinced that the Word (the Logos) extended itself over the whole world and beyond. One comes across this in the Parables. The Parables are cosmic. They have no real beginning nor any real end, neither time-wise nor space-wise (recalling Matthew 13:35: "I will open my mouth in parables; I will utter things which have been kept secret from the foundation of the world"). Each time we think we have come closer to a final understanding of the Parables, their horizon has receded. Yet in speaking about God's eternity,

Jesus has given His message in images derived from normal everyday life.

Ordinary everyday life is not ordinary. It cannot be measured and it cannot be assessed, precisely because the Kingdom of God is within us. Therefore, when speaking about everyday life, Jesus is speaking about much more than what we normally think. This makes the Parables so very awesome. In the Parables Jesus speaks about life without leaving out the essence of life, as we are wont to do. Our civilization has become so completely secularized that we no longer notice this deficiency in our observations and in our considerations of life.

In speaking about everyday life, Jesus has pointed to the deeper side of life, the real side of life. This deeper side comes to the surface when one tries to live as indicated in the Parables. It is man who buries this glorious kingdom under a layer of worldly wishes, worldly desires, as if the fulfillment of these desires would give lasting peace and satisfaction. Nowhere in the Parables is the fulfillment of these kinds of desires even mentioned. These desires impede the impact of the Kingdom of God. In this kingdom, One is King: God. And it is to Him that Jesus teaches us to pray as our Father. It is that prayer, so sacred that it should be prayed in one's closet because our Father is in secret (Matt. 6:6), which characterizes the link between God our Father and each of us. It is Jesus Who, with regard to this prayer, said that "thy Father which seeth in secret shall reward thee openly" (Matt. 6:6). And this brings us back to the Parables, where life is described as being visible to all of us. The Parables speak about the Kingdom of God, where it is and

what it is. Rejecting where Jesus said it is ("within you")
bars the road to understanding. And so it is perhaps not that
surprising that the Parables have not had any impact on the
formation of Christian doctrine.

In His Parables Jesus speaks about the Kingdom of God
in a specific way, a way defined by Jesus: "And he said unto
them, Unto you is given to know the mystery of the kingdom
of God: but unto them that are without, all these things are
done in Parables" (Mark 4:11). This way still is unexpected
for those who have grown up in the tradition of Christian
preaching. Not only is the length of the average Christian
homily so different from the length of the Parables. Far
more important is the following difference: In the Christian
sermon, the preacher is expected to explain, to give clear
expositions and statements in which man is explicitly
addressed. The question, however, is whether we are such
that we should be addressed that way.

In His Parables, Jesus speaks in symbolic language and
not in the kind of clear words and terms we are used to
hearing. Life is not what we can teach each other; life is
what man experiences in his own life, in sorrow and in joy.
It is through his experiences that man opens his heart. And
in this light one realizes that the Parables, which speak in
terms of everyday life, are given as a test to see whether we
put into practice what they teach us.

Jesus tells us in His Parables what we need, and what we
should do, in symbolic and, thereby, mysterious language.
To his disciples Jesus said that the mystery of the Kingdom
of God has been given (Mark 4:11). It is important to note
that in the Greek text of the Gospel of Mark, in contrast to

those of Matthew and Luke, it is not said that to the disciples it has been given to know the mysteries (plural) of the Kingdom of God. Rather it is the mystery (singular) of the Kingdom of God which has been given to the disciples. This singular gift does not function ex operato. This mystery of itself is not productive of spiritual effects without respect to the fitness, the willingness and the character of the recipient. Mark 4:13 makes this clear: "Know ye not this parable? and how then will ye know all parables?" The disciples are still in need of an explanation from Jesus. And that brings the hearer and the reader of the teachings of Jesus to two astounding awarenesses: that the Kingdom of God is within us, and that our lives have to be lived in such a way that we become aware that the Kingdom of God is within us. The teachings of Jesus in His Parables do not speak about believing—and certainly not in the way Christianity does—but about living for a certain, definite goal: coming closer, in life here on earth, to God.

Therefore it is not surprising that what we might call mere details in the stories of the Parables are not at all unimportant. Everything mentioned is of decisive importance for achieving that goal of coming closer to God. To achieve his goal, man must do something, man must do a lot, and that is taught in the Parables. Because the kind of life described in the Parables brings us to the cosmic reality of God, it would be preposterous to claim to have an overall view of the Parables. How can one ever have a general view of things eternal? When one reads a Parable, one discovers an abundance of differing elements which prohibits any attempt at generalizing. What the reader of the words of

Jesus can do is to try to enumerate the different and differing aspects of each Parable, aspects which are, in fact, existences of a rare diversity, each speaking in terms derived from human life about eternal life, about the Kingdom of God which is in man. Enumerating involves clear and precise thinking. The more this is done, the more one is guided by the Parables towards that reality, a reality which surpasses all our dimensions—both of thinking and living. This reality is a mystery, the reality which had been kept secret from the foundation of the world (Matt. 13:35). It is a mystery that the Kingdom of God, which is x-dimensional, is in us, who are 3-dimensional. The word "mystery" used by Jesus in relation to the Kingdom of God and its knowing (Mark 4:11) is linked with the word "all." The word "all" appears in the New Testament about 1,228 times, in the Greek Old Testament some 8,000 times. This word underlines the universality of the notion of God. It should not be forgotten that Jesus mentions the word "all" in connection with mystery.

Subsequent to the insights of Immanuel Kant we know that, when it comes to really knowing what things in themselves are, we know nothing. Kant also showed in his *Critique of Pure Reason* that God is, but that in His Eternal Being He cannot be known. However, in most conventional thinking, truth is still the adequacy between a thing and our knowledge of that thing. This misconception is of vital importance because Christian doctrine operates with this now-untenable presupposition, a legacy from Greek philosophy. In the face of what we nowadays know about the validity of our thinking, this presupposition, a cornerstone of

Christian doctrine, cannot be upheld. According to Albert Einstein, we can in our conclusions never go beyond tentative deductions. The whole idea that we can know things for what they are is a Western misconception. It cannot be linked to the Parables.

What a different society, and what a different and far-reaching knowledge we would have, had mankind not misled itself with the philosophical concept that we can know things for what they are. What a different Christian doctrine there would be today, what an amount of intolerance mankind would have been spared, had mankind not been hampered by that misguided philosophical concept and had better realized the importance and the necessity of thinking with regard to mystery. We would have seen what Einstein said: that for getting deeper insight we should have the freedom to give free reign to our fancy. According to Einstein, that is the only way for obtaining real insight. Einstein speaks about the link between thinking and believing. An awareness of this link would have spared our civilization its vast amount of atheism. According to Einstein, science without religion is lame, and religion without science is blind.

Understanding the limits of reason as identified by Kant and Einstein would also have made man more receptive to what mystery can be, so beautifully formulated by Albert Schweitzer when he said that the highest knowledge is that everything (all) that surrounds us is a mystery. No knowledge and no hope can give our lives stability and direction. Only to the extent that we let ourselves be taken by the ethical God, Who reveals Himself in us, and by surrendering our will to His, do our lives receive their firmness and certainty. It is a mystery that Jesus wants us to think about, and to act in accordance with, something that is in us and encompasses us. How did Jesus do this? To answer this question, one has to go to the most important source of information and ask: What did Jesus say about the Parables?

About His Parables, Jesus said that in them all these things "are done" for those who are not among His disciples; to His disciples it is given to know the mystery of the Kingdom of God. But because the Greek word for "given" (Mark 4:11) also means to be granted a request, those who are outside can come inside the circle of those who are close to Jesus when it is their sincere and heartfelt request to receive this gift from God. The circle of disciples, this text shows, is not a closed circle.

Again, Jesus said that in His Parables all these things "are done." Taking a closer look at the Greek word for "are done," one realizes that here much more is meant by "are done" than what one might normally think. With Greek, words often convey all sorts of related meanings. As is the case in Mark 4:11, "are done" reflects that when Jesus speaks, it is not just speaking as we do. It is not only predicating, describing. Words of man can do no more than that. But what Jesus speaks about, in Parables, actually comes into being, and this because of Him. One is reminded here of how it was said with grandiose simplicity: "And God said, Let there be light: and there was light" (Genesis 1:3); and it recalls: "For He spake, and it was done; He commanded and it stood fast" (Psalm 33:9).

It is remarkable that this basic aspect of the words of Jesus has not been mentioned by the Apostles, in the Epistles, in the Nicean Creed, or in the Apostles' Creed. "Are done" in Mark 4:11 also has the following connotations: to come into existence, to be born, to grow, to take place, to impart to a person, to come to a result. According to the text, all this is still happening. Nowhere is there any indication that the workings of this divine principle or entity will come to an end. And what is done? "All these things." And what are all these things? For that one has to listen to the Parables very carefully.

We have already noted that what the Parables bring is cosmic. How could it be otherwise, because Parables reveal things hidden "since the foundation of the world," or "since the foundation of all there is" (Matt. 13:35). This says something to us about the link between the Father and the Son. By saying "all these things," nothing is excluded by Jesus when He brought the Message of God. Human knowledge does not permit us to speak about "all," but it is exactly at that point, where man can realize his own limitations, that we can see the authority with which Jesus speaks, the authority which encompasses all.

All these things are conveyed to us in stories which seemingly deal with earthly situations only. But because these earthly situations are linked with all, linked with the mystery of which Jesus speaks, our life here on earth is not confined to life on earth. It stretches beyond that. How deeply that was felt and realized by Angelus Silesius when he said in his Cherubinic Wanderer: "The true Son of God is

Christ only, However every Christian has got to be the same Christ" (V, 9).

To be able to read more in the Parables implies coming closer to the Message of the Parables. To become essential, to seek the deeper side of life, to become what God has laid in us (Luke 17:21), to bring it to the surface of our lives—it is about all this that the Parables still speak. The Parables reveal the numberless aspects of the reality of the Father of Jesus, Who is also Our Father according to the teachings of Jesus. Or to say what the Parables tell us in the words of Angelus Silesius: "Of God nothing is known, He is the Only Existing One, What one knows of Him, that oneself has to be" (Cherubinic Wanderer, I, 285).

The way Jesus speaks about God is in contrast with the formulations of the Jews and Christians because the Parables do not argue about God, nor do they give the possibility for doing this. Here we see an amazing parallel: there is nothing in the Parables which characterizes God, although God is mentioned as a certain man or a certain rich man. What is there to argue about a certain rich man? This is very far away from the kind of arguing which flourished in the Middle Ages and afterwards with questions like: Can God create a stone which He cannot lift?

Such questions have troubled Christianity because they stem from the conviction that things can be known for what they are. That conviction has led toward ideas about God that are, to a very large extent, responsible for the religious crisis in which we are today. More and more people begin to ask themselves and others: Who is God? And they want an answer that will satisfy both hearts and minds. If religion

is going to survive in our western civilization, we should try
to be on the way towards a justified and well-founded belief
in God, justified and well-founded by the content of the
Parables. The teachings of Jesus do not justify our
preconceived ideas about God. In the light of this, it is not
that surprising to see that Christian theology has avoided
investigating the different concepts of God as they can be
found in the 66 books which together form the Bible. Very
little has been published in this vast area. And that is so
dangerous for the proper functioning of religion.

The religion of modern man stands and falls with ideas
about God. When one takes into account what modern man
knows about this world and the cosmos, problems arises as
to what one may think about a Being Who controls, from
moment to moment, every particle of reality in perhaps an
infinite number of universes. It is of the greatest importance
to notice that although God is mentioned in the Parable as a
certain (rich) man without any particularities, God does not
act like man (commending the steward, for example, in Luke
16). Therefore we do not have in the Parables an
anthropomorphic description of God. Man should not be
bound by all the ideas about God which cannot be traced
back to the Parables.

Modern scientific discoveries are not in opposition to
what the Parables teach about God; they are only in
opposition to what man has said about God in ages past.
Deeper understanding of the Parables will spare modern man
the otherwise unavoidable conflict between believing and
thinking. Precisely because there are no limiting views about
God in the Parables, it is the Parables which make it possible

for man to give free reign to his fancy when he is searching
for the Truth—a way of research advocated by Albert
Einstein.

It would be a denial both of the abundance and the
diversity of the content of the Parables to suggest that one
can ever master the subject. With the Parables the situation
is completely the opposite: the Parables master us and our
comprehension. When one tries to get to know what the
content of a Parable really is, one is reminded of astronomy:
in both cases one gets in contact with a reality which goes
beyond our horizon; and every time one feels that one might
have come closer to the horizon of a Parable, this horizon
gives way, recedes.

Thus what Jesus tells us is unceasingly open for further
understanding on our part. In this sense, one can say that
Jesus does not give us insight that we can use in the way we
typically handle our knowledge: as if it were final, as if it
were the last word. One should always realize that there is
a difference of principle between what Jesus says and our
understanding. First, there is the endless variety of content
in the words of Jesus. Secondly, there is the endless variety
of our understanding, not only with regard to the Parables,
but also with regard to everything else. This should make us
aware of a parallel between the Parables and the reality
(tangible reality included) in which we live. No aspect of
reality can be overmastered by us; we can never go beyond
tentative deductions in our acquiring of knowledge. This
parallel will not surprise us when we realize that God, the
Father of Jesus Christ, is the Creator of all there is. It is this
structural affinity in God, linking all there is, that helps us

to answer the question: Why did Jesus, when speaking about the Kingdom of God, do so in terms derived from ordinary everyday life? Jesus' use of those terms indicates that the real meaning of life is beyond terminology and beyond our interpretation of what life really is.

This structural affinity linking all, taught by Jesus when he said "The Kingdom of God is within you" (Luke 17:21), could have a stunning consequence: In our thinking we can participate in God's thinking about us. Paul in 1 Corinthians 2:16 points in that direction: "For who hath known the mind of the Lord that he may instruct him? But we have the mind of Christ." Again, according to Paul, this participating is not having full knowledge; full knowledge has to follow and will follow:

> For we know in part, and we prophesy in part.
> But when that which is perfect is come, then that which is in part shall be done away.
> When I was a child, I spake as a child, I understood as a child, I thought as a child; but when I became a man, I put away childish things.
> For now we see though a glass, darkly; but then face to face: now I know in part; but then shall I know even as also I am known.
> (1 Corinthians 13:9-12)

Our thinking has the possibility to be affected by that which is different from us, but with which we are linked. We form an integral part of reality, and man is different from what we think he is because of the Kingdom of God being within him.

Keeping this in mind, when one turns towards the Parables and sees again how Jesus spoke about the Kingdom of God, one realizes the vast importance of everyday life and the vast importance of our insights with regard to eternal life. There is more involved with man, more than we are used to accepting. Every word Jesus spoke to us has a content which goes beyond the content our words have. Jesus spoke to us from eternity, His origin being God's eternity. Our language is based upon the things of the earth, but the content of the words of Jesus has its basis in eternity.

Thus did Jesus say what the Kingdom of God is. One has to keep this in mind constantly when one reads the words of Jesus. The consequences of this disparity between the language of Jesus and that of ours has been put into words in a stringent way by Angelus Silesius: "What one knows of God that one has to be himself" (Cherubinic Wanderer I, 285). It is in the light of these profound words that one understands what Balthasar Munter has said: "I am allowed to contemplate Thee with reverence but to understand Thee I cannot."

# VIII.

Perhaps more than any other Parable, in the Parable of the Lost Son Jesus speaks about the Kingdom of God.

And he said, a certain man had two sons: And the younger of them said to his father, Father, give me the portion of goods that falleth to me. And he divided unto them his living.

And not many days after the younger son gathered all together, and took his journey into a far country, and there wasted his substance with riotous living.

And when he had spent all, there arose a mighty famine in the land; and he began to be in want.

And he went and joined himself to a citizen of that country; and he sent him into his fields to feed swine.

And he would fain have filled his belly with the husks that the swine did eat: and no man gave unto him.

And when he came to himself, he said, How many hired servants of my father's have bread enough and to spare, and I perish with hunger!

I will arise and go to my father, and will say unto him, Father, I have sinned against heaven, and before thee,

And am no more worthy to be called thy son: make me as one of thy hired servants.

And he arose, and came to his father. But when he was yet a great way off, his father saw him, and had compassion, and ran, and fell on his neck, and kissed him.

And the son said unto him, Father, I have sinned against heaven, and in thy sight, and am no more worthy to be called thy son.

But the father said to his servants, Bring forth the best robe, and put it on him; and put a ring on his hand, and shoes on his feet:

And bring hither the fatted calf, and kill it; and let us eat, and be merry:

For this my son was dead, and is alive again; he was lost, and is found. And they began to be merry.

Now his elder son was in the field: and as he came and drew nigh to the house, he heard musick and dancing.

And he called one of the servants, and asked what these things meant.

And he said unto him, Thy brother is come; and thy father hath killed the fatted calf, because he hath received him safe and sound.

And he was angry and would not go in: therefore came his father out, and intreated him.

And he answering said to his father, Lo, these many years do I serve thee, neither transgressed I at any time thy commandment: and yet thou never gavest me a kid, that I might make merry with my friends:

But as soon as this thy son was come which hath devoured thy living with harlots, thou hast killed for him the fatted calf.

And he said unto him, Son, thou art ever with me, and all that I have is thine.

It was meet that we should make merry and be glad; for this thy brother was dead, and is alive again; and was lost, and is found.

In the Parable of the Lost Son (Luke 15:11-32), more important than what the son does is what the Father does. This must have been difficult to understand for those who heard Jesus, as the Father does not act according to the belief of those days nor to present-day beliefs. The Parable explains what man can and, therefore, should do once man is entrapped in the temptations of the world.

The Father accedes to the rather unusual request of the younger son. The Father does more than is asked of him since he divides unto his two sons his living. Those hearing Jesus must immediately have realized that this Parable was not a story about what happens between earthly beings, as the Father, when dividing his living, is still alive. There is more about the Father which absolutely did not fit their concepts regarding God, concepts they had derived from the Old Testament. The Father runs to his son, something which represents, for us also, a different concept of God. The Father runs because he is exceedingly happy with his son's coming home. Why is the Father so happy? The Father, not the son, explains this: "for my son was dead, and is alive again, he was lost and is found." The Father is described by Jesus as being a deeply caring Father not only for his younger son, but also for his elder son, who is not rebuked for his unkind reactions, but invited to make merry with the Father.

It is also the Father who says what the younger son has gone through—that he had been "dead" and "lost." Nowhere do we read those words in the preceding verses, but apparently the situation of the lost son had been just that, one of death and loss. Being dead can be understood as being in a situation in which one is not aware of his link with God his Father, and this because of worldliness. Being alive can be understood as a state in which the son (i.e., man) is aware of this link. It is with the guidance of this awareness that man finds the way to his Father.

Jesus is speaking about time and eternity at the same time—the Greek words for "goods" and "living" in the first verse indicate this—and so the Parable encompasses life here and life hereafter. Jesus has made it known to his audience that the Kingdom of God is one in which man can be involved and can knowingly participate. That is extremely important, as illustrated by the actions of the Father. The link is a structural one. It forms part of the being of man. It can make man what he should be, as Angelus Silesius said:

> The divine Father-child relationship
> If God's divinity would not be closely in communion
>     with me,
> How then could I be His child and He my Father?
>                        (Cherubinic Wanderer I, 252)

The son was lost but was found. In his life, the son first loses everything. Then he realizes that he is lost, that nobody cares for him. For the son, therefore, the turning-point in his existence is to come to himself. At this turning-point, coming to himself, it also becomes clear that everything the son does receives its importance from the Father. The Greek word indicates that this coming to oneself is something that should be done not only once but continuously. Life is not what the son thought and expected it to be. Coming to himself tells us

that the son was searching for the deeper side of life. Or as
Angelus Silesius says in such an incisive way:

> To live outside of God is to be dead
> Man believe this for certain, where you do not live
> in God
> Even if you would live one thousand years, all that
> time you are dead.
>                               (Cherubinic Wanderer V, 111)

Most remarkable for us is that, after the son has come
home, the Father goes on showing His joy and expresses His
joy by ordering a festive meal with music. That God the
Father is that joyful because of the coming home of one
human being, His child, tells us, as does the rest of this
Parable, that the Kingdom of Heaven is very different from
what we are accustomed to think it is.

It is difficult for us for us to understand the behavior of
the older son, who has always been with the Father. The
Parable does not tell us whether he understood what the
Father said to him, thereby understanding his Father better
than he had done before. But the Father went out to entreat
him, also something that does not correspond with our
typical ideas regarding God.

This Parable therefore asks from us that we should try to
form a better idea regarding God than the idea we have now.
In fact, from beginning until end in this Parable, Jesus
interprets in human words a reality which is beyond human
words. In the sight of this Parable, the only thing we can say
is that Jesus has interpreted in human words what Jesus had
received from God. The message conveyed to us in this

Parable is inspiring and awesome at the same time. It is inspiring because the Parable shows us that the link with our Father is a living one which we can, and should, become aware of:

> The knower has got to become the known
> Of God nothing is known; He is different from all
>     there is;
> What one knows in Him, that one has to be oneself.
>                         (Cherubinic Wanderer I, 285)

The Parable is awesome in that it shows us that the responsibility for our conduct in life is ours, that each one of us has to find the way out of his or her trouble. That message is contrary to the attitude of present-day Christianity in which God is, in a sense, constantly asked to repair whatever we have broken. Far beyond the level of such requests, the Parable invites us to a level that is much different.

At the end of this Parable one cannot but remember what Angelus Silesius has said about God:

### The Unknown God

What God is no one knows. He is not Light, not Spirit,
Not Truth, Oneness, One, not what one considers Divinity
    to be.
Not Wisdom, not Intellect, not Love, Will, Goodness,
No Thing, no Phantasm, no Being, no innermost Sensitivity.
He is what I and you and all creatures who ever existed,
Before we have become what He is, never experience.
                        (Cherubinic Wanderer IV, 21)

# IX.

All the Parables speak about God, point to God. It might seem that man is in the center of the Parables, but since they speak about the Kingdom of God, they speak about its King. For this one has only to look at the Parables of the Lost Son and of the Unjust Steward. God is at the beginning and end of each Parable; without God man would lose his meaning and even his being. And so if man does not act as is taught in the Parables, how will he ever know God? This knowledge can be ours, if only the wish for acquiring it is focused on. The strength and the intensity of this wish is so beautifully described in Psalm 73:25: "Whom have I in heaven but Thee? And beside Thee I desire none upon earth." Jesus teaches in His Parables how to come closer to God and how to understand that only God is good and perfect. Nowhere in the Parables does anything appear of our way of speaking about God. That is because in Jesus' presence it becomes clear that there is in fact only one Teacher: God.

How then could one ever try to attempt to summarize the Parables? How could one ever think that man can summarize Who God is and what God does? How could eternal life ever be summarized? The Parables themselves do not present a summary. Each Parable speaks differently from the other Parables about God's eternity. Under the impact of the complexities of the Parables, one feels inclined to accept the insight of Anatole France that God's existences are of a rare diversity. This insight respects the endless complexity and pluriformity of the universe. The rare diversity of the aspects of eternity in the Parables is of an overwhelming abundance. Each aspect seems to be an entity of its own, in its own right. At the same time it appears that in a Parable each entity is closely interwoven with the rest. In this respect the Parable can be compared with a watch: every wheel is essential. When one mentions from a Parable only one aspect, immediately the rest is involved and needed for eventual understanding. Without any one of its elements, a Parable would be incomplete, and thereby would not function. All this has a bearing on what the situation of man really is; he too is intertwined with all that is; he too is a particle of God's reality. Here, as in astronomy, we see a much closer relationship between the cosmos and man than once thought. This link between man and the cosmos captured Einstein's full attention.

The organic linkage between eternity and man, pointed at in the Parables, was called by the Canadian psychiatrist R. M. Bucke a cosmic consciousness, an awareness of the situation being timeless. It is remarkable that Jesus, Who spoke to the multitude some 2,000 years ago and Who still speaks through His Parables to all of us, does not give any indication of time. Nor do the Parables ever indicate that they have been addressed to man because of some particular world situation. The Parable is valid always and for everyone. That could be the case because, according to the eminent scholar Hans Driesch, in the final analysis all subjects are one. This is in line with the statement of St. Augustine, that, in the final instance, "we and the Father are one." In a beautiful poem, the Calvinistic poet Jan Luyken said that he realized that God was the foundation of his foundation. His observation recalls the words of Jesus: "Know thyself; then thou willst be sons of the Father in Heaven, Who is perfect" (Oxyrrhynchos fragment). Thus the structure of the Parables shows us that nothing is outside the Kingdom of God. That, in its turn, could explain why the Parables have no beginning and no end. God's being is eternal; and the Parables, speaking about God, reflect eternity in their structure.

Where does the certain man in Luke 15:11 come from? Nothing is said about it, and this is also the case with regard to the certain rich man in Luke 16:1. In Luke 15:32 we see that the younger son was alive again after having been dead. Certainly, with regard to the Kingdom of God, the younger son is then in a situation without end. At the end of the Parable of the Unjust Steward (Luke 16), what is said about the steward? Nothing, because the serving of God has no end. The Parables tell us that man is surrounded by God's eternity and God's omnipresence. Texts such as "the kingdom of God is within you" (Luke 17:21) and "in him we live, and move, and have our being" (Acts 17:28) also bring this message to man. Man participates in a reality which is greater than he thinks it is. The teachings of Jesus presuppose this participation.

This relationship, a participation in a greater reality, is posited in the Parables. That relationship is always the starting point of a Parable. (It should be kept in mind that in this light a starting point is different from a beginning.) Then the Parables explain something about this relationship. Finally, the Parables tell us that what happens to this relationship is influenced by what we do. Precisely because the Parables speak about eternal life in terms derived from everyday life, one has to be searching constantly for the eternal meaning behind the words. All these earthly words in the Parables point to the fact that our life on earth has a deeper side. To live a worldly life is about the worst one can do. By realizing the deeper side of life on earth, one realizes more about the Kingdom of God. The relation between God and man has been mentioned by Calvin in a very impressive way: "experience testifies to it, that the seed of religion is laid in everybody." The immediacy of the religious consciousness comes from our origin (the kingdom of God within us), and this makes it possible for man to understand something of the vast and eternal importance of the Message of God given in the Parables.

It is exactly the mysterious haze, spread over the Parables, which warns man that he should desire to understand the Parables. And the way for understanding the Parables is given in the Parables themselves, not in the sense of understanding as an objective listener—but by becoming a participant in what has been given by Jesus. Or as Angelus Silesius has said: "Christian, where the Eternal God will take hold of thy heart, there should be in it no other image than that of His Son" (Cherubinic Wanderer, IV, 199).

Jesus' teachings were at the same time a doctrine; that is what the Greek text in Mark 4:2 tells us. What are we to think of the word "doctrine" when we meet this word in connection with His Parables? The presence of the word "doctrine," and its being connected with the Parables, tells us that what Jesus teaches is unchanging and therefore also the foundation for our coming closer to God. The word doctrine emphasizes that what Jesus teaches are the basic aspects of the Kingdom of God, which we should approach with trust and understanding. These characteristics are present in all Parables. In His doctrine Jesus speaks about life with God, eternal life. The use of the word "doctrine" in Mark 4:2 indicates that the Parables should not be ignored. Teaching His doctrine was the most important function when Jesus came to the multitude. The Parables are not fragments of Jesus' teachings. They contain His doctrine. All Jesus wanted to say to the multitude is to be found in the Parables.

Here we must ask: If the Parables, which seem to be nice little stories are, in fact, the way in which Jesus has given His doctrine, does this not force us to question the validity and the desirability of Christian doctrine? The result of hundreds of years of doctrinal theological thinking, Christian doctrine is so very different from the teachings of the Parables. What Jesus said encompasses life and the totality of things known by us; the words "all these things"—so closely related to totality—are characteristic of the teachings of Jesus and reveal the link between Jesus and His Father. In this one verse Jesus reveals Who He is.

In speaking about all these things with regard to the Kingdom of God, Jesus made His listeners aware that He is speaking about God. Jesus did this in such a way—by leaving out what we might call personality traits—that each and every one of us can have our own very personal and private concept of God. In this way the Parables tell us that since no two people are alike, no two people can have the same understanding of God. Therefore we should never force upon others our conception of God; we should never ever try to interfere with somebody else's understanding of God. Understanding, we have seen in the Parables, implies a relationship with God. Thus we begin to realize why Jesus accompanied His teachings with the instruction that one not judge other men and women (Matt. 7:1). With each of us God has a special and specific link. This link means that man should not make the big mistake of living as if he would stay here on earth forever, the big mistake inherent in a secularized outlook on life.

Life as it is described in the Parables prepares man for experiencing the end of his life here on earth, an end that is the call to eternal life hereafter, not as a blow but as an invitation. This is what man will find in the doctrine of Jesus. It is essential to see that had the Gospel not linked the word doctrine with the Parables, it would not have occurred to us that the Parables contain a doctrine. The word doctrine makes us think of an explanation which is characterized by its logical presentation. A doctrine, as we are used to understanding it, cannot be summarized in just one or two sentences. The presence of the word "doctrine" in Mark 4:2 should have prevented scholars from trying to summarize the Parables. Why has there not been the awareness that even the attempt to summarize eternity draws near the ridiculous; such an attempt looses sight of the proportion of eternity.

A doctrine—the word itself indicates this—is of such importance that it should not be left aside. But one sees, in the formation of Christian doctrine, that the doctrine of the Parables has been left aside. What would Christianity be today if the doctrine of Jesus would be its only doctrine? In explanations of the Christian faith the Parables do not have an essential and central place. Perhaps the strangest aspect of this development in history is how Christianity has actively built up its own many different doctrines next to the doctrine of Jesus, as if His doctrine were not there. It is dumbfounding to see how different from the doctrine in the Parables all of these doctrines are. How could Christianity ever convince itself, and remain convinced, that it would be permissible to have doctrines which, everyone can see for himself, are not the doctrine of Jesus? In His doctrine, for example, Jesus does not demand adherence to His doctrine, and that is in clear contrast to the attitude of Christianity.

Jesus in His Parables speaks about a way of life, a disciplined way of life. (The word doctrine is closely linked with discipline.) Evidently, coming closer to God and understanding more of God is not a matter of accepting doctrines made by man, but rather is a matter of a way of life, described in the various Parables, which encompasses man. This made the multitude realize that the authority of Jesus is unique. The doctrine of the Parables of Jesus speaks about life, eternal life, in such a way that the hearer realizes that he is not being taken by the hand and led by another mortal being. This approach contrasts exactly with what the priests and the scribes did, and their view on man was unfavorable: "But this people who knoweth not the law are

cursed" (John 7:49). Their method of leading the multitude
meant an immense power of the priesthood, a power
threatened by the content of the Parables. For the laity,
religion and priesthood became intermingled.[3]

On the other hand, Jesus teaches His doctrine with an
authority which cannot be compared with the one of the
scribes—to the astonishment of the multitude. The basis of
His doctrine and His authority is the relationship between
Jesus and God, His Father. The Gospel of Luke says: "His
word was with power" (Luke 4:32). It is this power which
made the multitude astonished. This power, this authority,
even impressed the temple police, as they themselves
testified. Apparently the authority they noticed in the
teaching of Jesus was also for them different from the
authority of the chief priests and the Pharisees. When asked
by the chief priests and the pharisees, they stated: "Never
man spake like this man" (John 7:45, 46). The Greek text
suggests that in the opinion of the temple police not only had
never anyone spoken like Jesus, but also no one ever will.
Why would the multitude and the temple police be that
impressed if they had heard before what Jesus said? Once
His authority is felt as the multitude felt it, one begins to
realize the ineptitude of human doctrine which, strangely

---

[3]The degree of misunderstanding of what religion is, and how
far that can lead, became clear in the French Revolution. A shrewd
and objective observer of the French Revolution, Madame de
Charrière, wrote in 1793 that the French believed they had
banished God through expelling the priesthood; Madame de
Charrière did not hesitate to qualify all this as the effect of temerity
over ignorance.

enough, always has been propounded as being final. Its human origin, however, makes such finality impermissible.

The more we realize that the doctrine of Jesus has its origin in eternity, the better we see how necessary it is that we do not assign any kind of finality to doctrines of our own. Whereas the Parables speak with final authority, today we know that our own conclusions never reach beyond the state of tentative deductions. Had this been known long ago, Christianity would have realized that there was neither room nor need for it to construct its own doctrines along side that of Jesus. It would not have lost sight that the Parables instruct us how to live and, as a result, how to come closer to God the Father. Also the dreadful conflict between believing and thinking that emerged in the 19th century, a conflict in which believing and thinking constantly intrude in each other's area, could not have arisen.

For us nowadays it is of utmost importance to see that our understanding of time, space, matter and energy no longer is the understanding of those who long ago formed Christian doctrine. Therefore: (a) insofar as Christian doctrine operates with now obsolete concepts, that doctrine has lost its validity; (b) the road is therefore now open for a better understanding of what Jesus said; (c) the Parables of Jesus, which speak with finality about life in the Kingdom of God, do not lend themselves to being measured with our unavoidably changing concepts of time, space, and reality. At the same time the character of our thinking, i.e., the unending process of investigating, shows that finality is something to strive for. Had this been realized long ago, Christianity could not have been saddled with the view,

allegedly coming from Tertullian (about 160-222 A.D.):
"Credo qui absurdum" (I believe because it is absurd).

The Christian religion, as the above may have made
clear, is in a deadly crisis. A Christian educator not so long
ago suggested not to build any more churches since in 50
years time churches will be empty. Christianity is entangled
in a deep conflict with present-day scientific thinking, and as
a result Christianity is suffocating in its own presuppositions.
The spiritual and intellectual descendants of Immanuel Kant
and Albert Einstein turn their back on the antiquated and
conventional answers and do not find in the current Christian
doctrine the peace the soul needs.

However, why not suppose that the Christian religion
would have an immense future if only it would conform
itself in teaching and living to the doctrine of Jesus (Mark
4:2)? Kant and Einstein have spoken about God, staying
remarkably consistent with the teachings of Jesus in the
Parables: In God man should have unlimited trust (Kant);
God is the illimitable superior spirit whose presence God
reveals in the incomprehensible universe (Einstein). It is with
this kind of understanding of God that man would no longer
have to face a conflict between religion and science. That
conflict forces many on the one side to accept what is
impossible to accept with the knowledge man has; on the
other side, the conflict forces man's thinking to try to impose
its dictates on that which is beyond the confines of his
knowledge. In the first instance, that is what organized
religion does; in the second instance, that is what atheism
does.

Of all the great philosophers of the West, Immanuel Kant is the only one who, in a systematic description of the possibilities of our acquiring of knowledge, has made clear that the Being of all beings, God, is the foundation of all that appears and that this Highest Being is absolutely unknowable. And in the Parables, which speak about the foundation of the world or cosmos, this foundation is elucidated in a way we would never think to do it. Angelus Silesius has beautifully described the limitations of our thinking and, at the same time, the mystery of the kingdom of God. "The more you know of God, the more you will admit, that the less you can say, Who He is" (Cherubinic Wanderer, V, 41).

Angelus Silesius made us mindful that what Jesus has given, kept secret from the foundation of the world or cosmos, does not have its origin in our world, but in the being of God. This is done, to our surprise, in examples derived from everyday life. Not only do the Parables show us the importance of our everyday life, they also show that our everyday life has got to become more like life as illustrated in the Parables. Man's life has to be perfected; man has to become perfect. For this man has to become essential as God is essential. Then man will understand Mark 4:11: "And He said unto them, Unto you it is given to know the mystery of the kingdom of God: but unto them that are without, all these things are done in parables." For coming closer to this mystery one has to come closer to perfection.

In His Parables Jesus spoke in such a way that no one who listened to Jesus would ever get the idea that he could understand Jesus in the way we think we understand reality.

Of course, we do not see this as long as we think that with our conceptual thinking we can understand the Parables. Many theologians have thought they could do this, and thus they have been far from happy with Mark 4:11. Carl Clemen, for instance, stated without any further elucidation that Mark 4:11 is not authentic. Albert Schweitzer—and he is not the only scholar to make this mistake—went so far as to say that Jesus only "sometimes" spoke in Parables in order not to be not understood. The way Jesus spoke prevents us from ever supposing that we can adequately understand the Parables and, thus, be able to adequately assess what Jesus said. This way of teaching by Jesus indicates to us that it is not only via our human understanding that we will receive access to God and His eternity, but also through becoming perfect.

In the Parable of the Unjust Steward, for instance, the road to perfect life is given: "the Lord commended the unjust steward" (Luke 16:8). With our understanding and thinking we would never have spoken about God as we read in the Parable—a warning not to follow the path of atheism where a constant mistake is made: thinking that reality is what we think it is. This mistake should not be made any longer since Immanuel Kant proved that access to reality by pure thinking is not given to man.

With our understanding and thinking, we would never have spoken about being perfect the way Jesus did. The Parables speak about the Kingdom of God. They speak about being perfect because they speak about eternal life with God, Who is perfect. They speak about being perfect because they speak about life towards God. "Towards" God? Is that really enclosed within the meaning of the word "perfect"? The word perfect includes the meaning of "arrived at the end, reached the end." But because Jesus said that we should be perfect even as our Father in heaven is perfect, this end is therefore eternal. Only One is eternal; only One is; all the rest has a derived existence from the only One Who is: God. He is, for us, the end.

Exactly because the Parables speak about the Kingdom of God or about the Kingdom of Heaven, they therefore speak about eternity and about the road towards eternity. Because in the Parables Jesus speaks about the link between man and eternity, the Parables do not show us the picture of man that is prevailing in our time. It is we who are astonished (to say the least) about texts like Mark 4:11, where God's eternity is not open to man's typical way of understanding. God's eternity can be found when our lives will be in conformity with the attitude in life as described in the Parables, an attitude which enables us to see through the many interests of this world and which makes us aware that our soul aspires to God alone.

In the teachings of Jesus, the goal of each and every man is to come closer to God, not through (logic) reasoning and (logic) arguing, but through living the kind of life as described in the Parables. A beautiful example of this is found in the behavior of the Unjust Steward. The houses, the hearts of men, have become through the behavior of the Unjust Steward everlasting habitations, temples of eternity. Since only God is eternal, these hearts have become temples of God. As long as our hearts have not become temples of God, the Parables will be for us inaccessible.

As long as we do not realize that it is through our everyday life that it should become manifest that God is Almighty, Omnipresent and All-pervading, we thereby close the road to the deeper and real side of life. Or as Angelus Silesius put it: "What one knows in God, that one has to be oneself" (Cherubinic Wanderer, I, 285).

In His Parables Jesus gives man the possibility of becoming an active part of the Kingdom of God. His indwelling Word can make this for us our deepest desire, and we can begin to see how St. Justin Martyr could say that Jesus Christ is the personal form of appearance of the Logos (Word), which dwells in every man. To try to understand this in an objective and non-involved way, that is, as if it were something we are not closely linked with, would be totally erroneous. Angelus Silesius said in his own inimitable way: "The true Son of God is Christ only; However every Christian has got to be the same Christ" (Cherubinic Wanderer, V, 9).

This indwelling brings us closer to why it is that Jesus would speak about mystery while mentioning man's everyday life. This way of teaching shows Jesus' divine authority. At the same time Jesus impresses upon His hearers the link that exists between Him and them, a link which guides man through his life here on earth, a link which remains shining on the path of man. It is the Word of God, in the specific appearance of Jesus, which makes it possible for man to see the path through life. The Parables are formulated in such a way that man can be sure that this guidance towards the ultimate goal of life, God, is always there.

No doubt it is a mystery, and the Gospel of Mark stresses that the teachings of the Gospel are a mystery. Jesus spoke about things which have been kept secret from the foundation of the world. When reading Jesus' Parables one has to ask oneself: Who is He, Who comes to me in His Words now? It is this coming of Jesus to us that makes us mindful that the words of His Parables are more than human words. The words of Jesus effectuate what they convey.

The light of the Parables make it possible for us to see through ourselves, our believing, our thinking, our acting. What do we see? Instead of trusting in these words of Jesus, man has constructed systems which, he thinks, will bring mankind to a better world. Through systems man has thought he would get a reliable grip on the reality by which he is surrounded. In the area of religion this has led, for instance, to the Inquisition, a horrendous consequence. Secularized forms of this bent of the human mind have been found in systems which have tried to conquer society (e.g., communism and fascism) and which can never function without intolerance and without the gruesome and inhuman curtailing of man's freedom of believing and thinking. Freedom for progress in these areas has been pointed to by Albert Einstein when he spoke of the need of giving free reign to one's fancy. Systematizing reality is an attempt man should never make. A system is a set arrangement of things so related or connected as to form a unity or organic whole. Who would like to have the temerity to say that God's creation can be handled by doing just that? Who would like to be so bold as to maintain that, through systematizing, man (with his background) can be known (and thereby guided,

forcibly or not) for what he really is? Let it not be forgotten
that systems have the tendency to treat the unknowable with
minute precision. Systems exercise on man attraction and
flatter him since they are for him the brackets on which he
can put his knowledge on display. Remembering this would
make us less intolerant. Systems make us forget precisely
that we do not have the possibility of making overall views.
This is definitely true with regard to the Kingdom of God.

And so the Parables do not provide us with any kind of
systematic approaches to the Kingdom of God and to the
world. The Parables show through examples what the
Kingdom of God is, and this is done by also pointing at man.
This is awesome and a source of unending thankfulness.
Nowhere do the Parables teach constraint as we know it.
What we find big and important is not present in the
Parables: "That which is highly esteemed among men is
abomination in the sight of God" (Luke 16:15). The
improvement of man, and the situation in which man lives,
does not come from outside man, i.e., through religious or
political systems, but from within, where the Kingdom of
God is (Luke 17:21). The Parables lead man towards the
way which also leads to an improvement of our world.

It is the doctrine of Jesus which sets us free, most of all
free from ourselves. And so the Parables lead us towards a
natural life. A natural life is a life in which one realizes his
link with God. When one does just that, one wants to
become essential, since this link becomes for him more and
more essential. The Parables show man the way. It is a way
upwards which makes us leave behind the density of the
world. It is a way which leads towards God.

Reading and rereading the Parables will change our understanding of the Parables constantly. It will direct our deepest desires towards the background of man, where man comes from, his Source. And so the Parables close the circle of our existence. It was exactly this which made Angelus Silesius say at the end of his Cherubinic Wanderer: "Friend it is enough. In case you want to read more, Then go and become yourself the Scripture and the Essence."

# INDEX

A Note about the Author


HENDRIK VAN TUYLL VAN SEROOSKERKEN is professor emeritus of philosophy and religion at the University of Montevallo and a resident of Mountain Brook, Alabama. He holds the Th.D. degree from the state university at Utrecht, The Netherlands. His dissertation focused on the *Critique of Pure Reason* in the philosophy of Immanuel Kant. He is an ordained deacon in the Church of England and a minister of the United Church of Canada. For two years Dr. van Tuyll was assistant professor of philosophy at Acadia University in Nova Scotia. He taught at Montevallo from 1966 to 1981. The author of a previous monograph, "Problems Concerning the Portraits of J. S. Bach," he is completing work on a new book that examines little-known origins of early Christianity.

If you enjoyed this book...

We hope that you will either pass it along or purchase copies for your friends. Middle Street Communications strongly encourages readers to support their local booksellers. The service these businesses provide in making available important works such as *The Parables:* **The Forgotten Message** is invaluable. This book is available through major wholesalers, so your bookstore should be able to get additional copies if none are currently in stock.

However, if you need to order by telephone, you may use a credit card and call **1-800-444-2524, ext. 169**. This number is available 24 hours a day. Please note that the 800 number is for **orders only**. Have your card ready when you call. The cost is $9.95 plus $3.75 shipping for the first copy, $1.50 shipping for each additional copy. (The fax number for credit card orders is 813-753-9396.) If you prefer to order by mail, you can save shipping charges. Send your name, a complete address, and a check or money order for $9.95 to:

Middle Street Communications
P. O. Box 223
Pelham, AL 35124-0223

Finally, we always welcome your insights. If you have comments regarding this book or any other publications from Middle Street, just send us a note at the address listed above.